Around the Corner

Reflections on American Wars, Violence, Terrorism, and Hope

By John W. Davis

Author of *Rainy Street Stories*

AROUND THE CORNER

Reflections on American Wars, Violence, Terrorism, and Hope

By John W. Davis

AUTHOR OF *RAINY STREET STORIES*

Around the Corner-Reflections on American Wars, Violence, Terrorism, and Hope

Published by: Red Bike Publishing
Copyright © 2021 by John W. Davis

Published in the United States of America
www.redbikepublishing.com

Red Bike Publishing also publishes books in electronic format. Some publications appearing in print may not be available in electronic book format.

Library of Congress Control Number: 2018932427
ISBN: 978-1-936800-32-2

This book is dedicated to my wife, Jane, who went with me around the corner.

For my sons, Marty, Will, and Kenny
    ---With all my love.

Horatio:
O day and night, but this is wondrous strange!

Hamlet:
And therefore as a stranger give it welcome.
There are more things in heaven and earth, Horatio,
Than are dreamt of in your philosophy.

--William Shakespeare, **Hamlet**, Act 1, scene 5, 159–167

Travel is fatal to prejudice, bigotry, and narrow-mindedness, and many of
our people need it sorely on these accounts. Broad, wholesome, charitable
views of men and things cannot be acquired by vegetating in one little
corner of the earth all one's lifetime.

– Mark Twain, **Innocents Abroad**

The cover art, a pen and ink original titled, Around the Corner, is by my oldest son Marty.

Photography by Terri Davis

CONTENTS

GRATITUDE AND ACKNOWLEDGEMENTS

My career as an investigator of espionage and terrorist cases for the US Army was governed by two concepts. The first is that "Life is infinitely stranger than anything the mind of man could invent," as Sir Arthur Conan Doyle said. Secondly, I've always believed Russian author Fyodor Dostoyevsky's observation, "Nothing is easier than to denounce the evildoer; nothing is more difficult than to understand him." I want to thank those institutions of learning which introduced me to these writers, and to a host of other thinkers. I'm a graduate of William Cullen McBride High School and Washington University in St. Louis, Missouri, so I thank those great schools and their wonderful educators for guiding me to an intriguing career of mystery and languages. My stories of people and events I encountered as a result are true, and often stranger than anything I could make up. These revelations about the human condition bear greatly on our common search for justice. I hope you too can reflect on these tales in light of your own experiences.

To offer thanks to all of those who helped me in this effort is daunting. I'd like to begin by thanking my wife Jane, whose good humor kept a home and our family together while we were constantly on the move both overseas and in America. We have three wonderful sons, Marty, Will, and Kenny. They are my joy, and their encouragement to go together on many 'mighty adventures' made our life one of true happiness.

I've countless colleagues from European and American intelligence and police services to thank, and for their understanding, professional guidance, and honesty I will forever be grateful. My military and police friends from various services and nations should be recognized also for their camaraderie and helpfulness in understanding what being a good soldier and an effective investigator means. Every spouse and family member of my associates is more of a patriot than we'll ever be able to honestly express. I want to recognize as well my colleagues in academia, whose intensive researches introduced me to dimensions of human nature I'd never have known otherwise. All of these people made this book possible. Thank you all.

So too I want to thank our friends who are now part of an open world where once a giant Iron Curtain separated us. Thank you all for your openness, frank appraisals, and kindness to my family. Likewise, through the wonderful efforts of the non-profit organization Global Ties, Alabama, we've made many new friends from every continent. These vibrant young representatives of the world's nations helped fashion and greatly influenced my belief that going around the corner, and not being afraid of one another, is the most important step we can take in our life. It is how peace among nations can come about.

Every person mentioned in this book, Billy, the Gray Fox, Leo Sassen, Dan, Renate and Georg, Werner and a host of others know they are loved. Those whose names I cannot mention are always in my heart, if not in the written word.

Many of the essays and poetry in this book were published in hallmarks of professional journalism. Thank you to The SOHO Journal in Manhattan, The Decatur Daily, AL.com, ARMY Magazine, the Valley Planet, the Athens News Courier, Clearancejobs.com, The Military Intelligence Bulletin, Mysterious Writings, Cengage Corporation, English Teaching Professional Magazine, The Federation of American Scientists, The Officer Journal of the Reserve Officers Association, and a host of others. My friends, Jeff Bennett owner and senior editor at Red Bike Publishing, reviewer John Cummings, and linguistic master Gray Sutherland all kept me on target and encouraged. My fellow writer Ricky Thomason was always there to lend a wise ear, advice, and friendship. Any errors, of course, are mine alone.

No amount of thanks can suffice to make clear how much my wife Jane, our sons Marty, Will, and Kenny helped me to remember, to understand, and again to share the joys and wisdom that come from a life well lived together. I offer all my friends, and especially my family, all my love.

When I left home at the beginning of thirty-seven years' service with the US Army and the secret world, my dad, Bill V. Davis, gave me a keepsake. It was a copy of Rudyard Kipling's poem, 'If'. I found the poem's encouragement to practice patience, to be considerate, balanced, and to spend some time in a certain humble, thoughtful reflection helped me in life. It became an ideal to pursue, and a major influence on my book.

If
By Rudyard Kipling

If you can keep your head when all about you
    Are losing theirs and blaming it on you,
    If you can trust yourself when all men doubt you,
  But make allowance for their doubting too;
If you can wait and not be tired by waiting,
  Or being lied about, don't deal in lies,
Or being hated, don't give way to hating,
  And yet don't look too good, nor talk too wise:

If you can dream—and not make dreams your master;
  If you can think—and not make thoughts your aim;
If you can meet with Triumph and Disaster
  And treat those two impostors just the same;
If you can bear to hear the truth you've spoken
  Twisted by knaves to make a trap for fools,
Or watch the things you gave your life to, broken,
  And stoop and build 'em up with worn-out tools:
If you can make one heap of all your winnings
  And risk it on one turn of pitch-and-toss,
And lose, and start again at your beginnings
  And never breathe a word about your loss;
If you can force your heart and nerve and sinew

To serve your turn long after they are gone,
And so hold on when there is nothing in you
 Except the Will which says to them: 'Hold on!'

If you can talk with crowds and keep your virtue,
 Or walk with Kings—nor lose the common touch,
If neither foes nor loving friends can hurt you,
 If all men count with you, but none too much;
If you can fill the unforgiving minute
 With sixty seconds' worth of distance run,
Yours is the Earth and everything that's in it,
 And—which is more—you'll be a Man, my son!

PROLOGUE

Still round the corner there may wait, a new road or a secret gate.
--J.R.R. Tolkien, English author

I've always been fascinated by mystery; I've always wanted to know what was around the corner. 'Around the corner': the phrase itself has mysterious, inviting, and even sinister meanings. In the Roaring 20s, the Germans had an expression, '*um die Ecke bringen*', which means 'to bring around the corner'. It was used when they meant to have someone killed. For many people, content where they are, to imagine going around a corner is a chance they'd rather not take. As suggested by the insidious expression *um die Ecke bringen*, going somewhere unknown tapped into the most visceral human fear of all, the fear of the unknown. Great men as diverse as Edmund Burke, the 18th century British parliamentarian, and President Franklin Delano Roosevelt of our country, perceived that it was fear itself that brought about paralysis of action, and forced a reluctance to try another way. A corner meant something new and unexpected. Some feared even to venture a look, others not. Some remained enwrapped in their parochialism - not to say provincialism - because it protected what they knew and loved. Others ventured around to see what life offered beyond the known.

In the old neighborhood where I was born in north St. Louis, Missouri, ranks of pale red-brick houses shouldered others for block after block. Every few streets defined a new language, indeed a different culture. An entire way of life could change in every short distance you walked. As I grew older, I came to realize that many people feared such changes, or any change at all for that matter, even if it was just down the street. They were afraid of the strange and the unknown, just around the corner. Difference meant uncertainty, which implied chances rather not taken. For me, taking a chance to see what might be beyond the known, safe, and visible was overwhelming. I paced miles along the railroad tracks which began only eight houses from mine. Along those mesmerizing, endless creosote soaked wooden ties, over steep viaducts with tucked away hobo sleep niches, past the acrid sulphur plant and its 'shotgun slinger' old geezer guard, ranks of back yards and piles of strange, unexplored debris I relentlessly, but with greater awareness, walked on.

Who were these distant concentrations of people, some of whom didn't even speak English? New and memorable brick buildings seemed shoved right up to the tracks. Dodging great rust and black locomotives huffing through the oddly attired people living in the vast, cramped city was a strange sort of game. Only once was I caught, Keystone Kops movie-like, standing in the middle of a long viaduct with only ties, rails, and supports. A whistling train pumped toward me like Hell's horses. It was too far to run back. It was too far to plunge ahead? Jump? I made a leap for it, a semi slide really, landing luckily without breaking a bone on the support brace. Cuts I could handle, the laughing kids down by the pick-up ball field no. I also avoided the occasional 'railroad dick' whose job seemed to be chasing kids from the tracks. (Did one really wear a bowler hat and scruffy tweed coat?) Even odd, greasy, gasoline tinged or appealing smells arose during these journeys through my small but expanding world. Always, yes always something scary, fun, dangerous, downright weird, unknown, or noteworthy appeared as I wandered past block after block after block. I went through gigantic, lonely but wonderful and haunting Calvary Cemetery to neighborhoods known to me only by name. I walked down miles of city streets just to see. I had to know.

As I listened to stories of older relatives and neighbors, I gradually became of aware of entire worlds beyond the block. It seemed at once populated by friendly enough people, or dangers beyond imagination. And so tensions grew in my life. I wanted to see for myself beyond the known and the secure. I wanted to visit places described by old Billy when he went to France in the Great War. I wondered later about my wife Jane's dad, who had fought in Europe during the Second World War, and how that war, communism, democracy, and fascism influenced much of my life. With the chance to be engaged in the sinister secret world of the Cold War, I found myself in a place where going 'around the corner' carried life impacting significance. Indeed, I discovered in my own life the unknown drew me like a siren's song.

These reflections are what I discovered when I decided to go 'around the corner'. I hope you find these stories of personal encounters, actual dilemmas, strange events, and a panoply of aspects of human nature as intriguing and thought provoking as I did.

What did it all mean?

INTRODUCTION

Once men are caught up in an event they cease to be afraid. Only the unknown frightens men.--Antoine de Saint-Exupéry

All intelligence is trying to see around a corner. The secret world is made up of people who try to discover what is just beyond their sight. Where the seeker cannot go, he must create one who will act on his behalf. Thus we enter a strange world, with locutions like cutout, asset, monitoring devices, surveillance, and spies. To properly employ such, of course, brings us to an unexpected new dimension. Now we approach the realms of truth, honesty, law, and ethics, and their obverse of lies, betrayal, compromise and ego. No one, the saying goes, gets a free pass from right or wrong. Even in pursuit of a secret adversary, we in the Western traditions follow laws. Either we obey the law ourselves or we become what we claim to oppose. That is to say unless, of course, one believes might makes right. Unless your practices are those of a police state, or of true believers, who believe all virtue lies on their side, you follow the law to defend your own way of life. Let me cite one story as an illustration.

There was a US Army sergeant in World War II, a Jewish soldier who joined the OSS, the precursor of the CIA, and jumped behind German lines. Captured by the Gestapo, he was tortured terribly. After the war, he chanced to encounter the very man who had tortured him. The Gestapo man was in a prison, and he cowered into a corner when the OSS man entered. The Nazi begged that the Americans would not torture his wife and child. With a puckish grin, the OSS man said, "Don't worry. We aren't Nazis."

Our seeker in the secret world often can't go around the corner himself because dangers await him in forbidden zones. Around the corner could be a police state, which would murder an inquirer as easily as take him captive. Poison, falls from windows, or plane crashes characterize this silent application of evil. Or the land beyond could be populated by true believers, whose bizarre rites take the shape of torturing, lynching, burning or decapitating their non-believing victims. Or the state might be yours or mine, a liberal democracy, which to protect itself has laws, regulations, and custom. All of these systems must protect themselves. How they do so is what separates one from the other.

After some four years as an artillery officer in the 101st Air Assault Division, I entered the secret world. My new job was to learn languages and catch spies. My European colleagues were often a generation older than me. They had lived through the Second World War. A couple had been in the Resistance against Nazi occupation. I was astounded to discover how much that last war still impacted our lives, and my professional life. As time went on, we went after terrorists, too. Ours was a world where we'd try to understand such threatening people by living their lives vicariously. "If I were a spy, and wanted to know this, how would I go about it?" "What would a terrorist do in such circumstances, believing what he does?"

We could study others, or interview them, the better to understand them. Then we in counterintelligence would set about defending ourselves against the spies or terrorists. Such defenses changed over time. New technologies ensured this happened. Where once a paid informant helped, now computers did much of the work. Nevertheless, money, ideology, compromise and ego remained the general motivations for most spies and terrorists in this duplicitous world. Betrayal was driven by one or another.

It was the true believer who was hardest to understand and defeat. Where once he believed in the god of a communist Utopia just around the corner, now he might as well believe in a Caliphate, national resurgence, or white supremacy, to name but three. The true believer hoped to restore a once idyllic past, which had been corrupted. In all such cases, these proponents spoke of their imagined future as free of all pain, corruption, duplicity, and evil. And everyone would finally belong, and be recognized, once all the evil, corrupt and corrupting enemies of the people, their class, party, religion or race had been destroyed. The wondrous world to come on Earth was the pure vision for which the true believer fought. No crime that would serve to bring about this Nirvana in the flesh was too debased for this noble crusader, the true believer. The beatific, earthly end justified all means, any means at all. And that world was just around the corner, once all the corrupt evil-doers were killed. These fantasies motivated the true believer. He believed. He too, was on a journey around the corner, but carried a bomb.

As time passed, the Cold War passed into its bloody, chaotic aftermath. Places like the former Yugoslavia dissolved into inter-religious bloodbaths. The Middle East exploded as wars begat wars. Such a world was affected by our own country, which in turn was affected by it in an endless cycle. A trained intelligence officer, however, could not help but observe as dispassionately as possible. I write also of how our society seeks clarity in such a post-Cold War world.

And of course, our metaphor about seeing around a corner doesn't end here. We have many opportunities to see around corners, particularly in times of peace. But we ban ourselves from doing so. We don't as a rule encourage foreign-language study. I dare say we invaded Iraq, a country the size of California, with only some forty-three fully qualified Arab linguists assigned to our entire Army.

Thus we prevent anyone but those who speak English from first-hand communication with us. We make ourselves beholden to those who speak the foreign tongue and translate it for us. We trust foreign translators who may, or may not, have our interests at heart. I recall a young man, a native of the land we occupied, who had to remain in his country after we left. His language skill, which had been so helpful to us, was his death sentence among those who came after we left.

I discuss language capabilities at some length, because human lives are at risk where we don't have such skills. We can better serve our country if we improve them. After all, it was a certain proficiency in foreign languages that brought about my career as a foreign intelligence linguist, liaison officer, and investigator. Lest we forget, the most important part of language use is listening. This is not a skill Americans are renowned for. The humility, patience, and listening that come with learning a foreign language, learning to speak first as a child with others my own age, served my later mission to preserve and protect our nation as well. A certain humility serves one well who needs empathy for others.

Perhaps another prohibition we impose on our abilities to see around a corner is arrogance. "We know, you don't." Thus we impose our rules on people we barely knew about a month before. We expected those we encountered to cherish values that had taken us many generations, a different history, and indeed wholly separate religious and social experiences to develop. Lincolnian equality and Jeffersonian democracy are not widely shared or understood outside America or a few other lands. We must learn to listen to what others say, and perhaps learn something from them.

Prejudice can keep us from knowing what is there for all to see. As Sir Arthur Conan Doyle's Sherlock Holmes commented to his erstwhile friend Dr. Watson, "You see Watson, but you do not observe." Add to this our American impatience, and you have failure staring at the cliff's edge. What investigation is favored by prejudging the evidence, and impatiently expecting preordained, too quick results? I hope to show how those practices which succeeded in my foreign service can help our nation as we deal with our own histories of racial discord and violence. Indeed, what police efforts can succeed if people who would report crimes see the police not as a friend but as the enemy? Was it not General U.S. Grant who said it simply, "The art of war is easy enough. Find out first where the enemy is." Why do people take up guns to shoot others, in schools, in foreign countries, in positions of authority, or even in our churches? When we find out the answer to these questions, we are well on our way to finding out where the enemy is. The best defense against violence in neighborhoods is to build community, where the police and all citizens, regardless of their background, help one another because they perceive themselves as Americans.

What makes us strong as a nation is unity of purpose. If we cannot make all Americans, of whatever heritage, feel a part of our common liberty, *e pluribus unum*, we violate our own foundation. You cannot build on a bed of sand. You certainly can't do it by force, prisons, police, and surveillance. We have more than enough models of eastern European Communist failure to demonstrate that. If we can't see around the corners of our own towns, observe and understand through patience and listening, we are lost. We'll never understand our youth, our own people, if we don't give them the same respect we'd hope for in return. I write to assert we can succeed, and to show where we have done so. I feel obligated to tell these true stories, because they reveal what is best about our country, or where not, where we can make a strength of our ability to learn anew.

PART I: INFLUENCES

Si propius stes, Te capiet magis. The closer you stand, the more you see.-- John Dryden, 17th Century English Poet Laureate, ***Absalom and Achitophel***

Just keep a good attitude!--Said by a stranger at a rest stop on Highway I-55, in 1975, when asked what I owed him for fixing my car in the middle of the night.

BILLY

Two huge Irish setters knocked the old man down. My friend and I dropped our book bags and ran to help him. As we rushed across the street, we heard him laughing.

"Don't be mad at the dogs, boys. I called them over so I could pet them. These old legs of mine couldn't hold up to their friendliness."

That's how I met my friend Billy. We walked back with him to the old folk's home, the *Altenheim*, in the former German settlement of Baden in north St. Louis, about a block away. He invited us in. Everybody smiled, waved and greeted him. He joked and had a congenial comment and a wink for everyone. His room was tiny. There was a bed, a desk, chair, a washbasin and a toilet. But the walls and desk drawers were filled with pictures, paintings, and photographs of an amazing life. Billy had a story for each one of them.

Throughout my high school and college years I visited Billy often. He told colorful stories of his life as a cowboy in Wyoming. Then there were news clippings of Billy on an oil derrick in Oklahoma. He even prospected for gold in Idaho and Montana. "We could move around and do anything. That's freedom," Billy said. "I joined the army before the Great War. Kaiser Bill gave me my first chance to see Europe. That's me and my boys there." The old sepia photograph hung framed near the window. In it the faces of a hundred or so Doughboys stared out at me from a moment in time in 1917. "Which one is you, Billy?" "That one, in the middle," he smiled. Of course, there was Billy, seated Indian fashion in the front and center. As always, he was smiling. His twinkling younger eyes made the photo seem to come alive. He was an infantry captain in the American Expeditionary Force of Black Jack Pershing. I was looking at the company of soldiers he took to war.

He and his men took part in the great Meuse-Argonne offensive in France. "Many of my friends never came back from France. They lie there beneath the sod." Interesting that he called them friends.

"Maybe someday you'll get to visit France, Johnny. It's such a beautiful country."

Time went by. I visited Billy and the seasons passed. He told me of his family, now grown, and of his fondly remembered wife, now dead. He joined in singing with the visiting school choir at Christmas and regretted he could no longer play soccer with the children in the schoolyard next door when spring came around. "I think they'd pick me last now," he joked. This is not to say he didn't try! Once I saw him out there in the playground, in the game, quite forgetting he was ninety two years old.

Each spring I particularly remember Billy, and his immense joy of life. He was only sad once that I recall. I neared college graduation and its attendant worries. "I wish all young people could live like I lived. We were so free and happy."

As the years passed I did get to visit France. With my own wife and boys I visited the pastoral American cemetery where the thousands of dead of the Meuse-Argonne offensive are buried. Beneath the giant, silent oak sentinels, the cool breeze of May made the grasses ruffle against the white marble crosses. Here others, now gone, who once knew Billy as I did, lie buried 'beneath the sod.' They knew him when they were the same age as I was, although we were separated by some two generations. What greater evidence of the invisible bonds of memory which bind generations together could I hope to experience? This place that Billy remembered is now a part of mine. It occurred to me that such a place of placid tranquility is something he never experienced while here. It is a testimony to his infectious optimism that he spoke of France's beauty, nevertheless.

I'll never forget Billy, William Bischoff. He was happy, kind and a true friend. He grew old graciously and was fun to be around. He shared his memories of what life was like before I lived. That is a gift worth having, and in turn, sharing.

Offerings *was inspired through my acquaintance with Billy Bischoff. He recalled once how he so missed those of his company of soldiers he left 'under the sod' in France in 1918. He hoped someday I would see France. I did. This is my memorial to him and those still there, 'under the sod.'*

OFFERINGS

Crowded together, stamping boots, white breath or cigarette smoke wafting out from under rain clicking tin helmets,

We waited for the word in that trench.

The old timers knew if you held your top button over your nose, and breathed directly on your skin,

There was a sensation of warmth.

It lasted but a second or two, but overwhelmed even the spears in stiffened toes, and stopped shivers for a precious while.

Someone said we inhabited the smallest chapel of all, in that trench.

A spare moment of thought might slip past the aches, the ever sucking mud, and our dried, sticky sweat's clamminess.

Men thought. About God, or maybe not. Waiting.

Fear of what awaited 'over the top' might dissolve into a cigarette puff's nothingness, or into heaves, or unstoppable shakes.

Everyone hoped the agony would be over in an instant.

We heard, out there, beyond the wire, as the other side cocked their bolts, resting their waiting offerings of lead into their chambers.

The wind which bore that sound would soon carry the incense of poison gas our way, too.

Our officer, vested in trench coat, mask hanging free, chambered his pistol. We loaded as well.

"Meet you on the other side, boys!"

This is my body.

"Over the top!"

With a whistle we climbed a makeshift ladder, clumps of mud falling, boots slipping, and crossed over.

This is my blood.

THE GRAY FOX

We called him the Gray Fox. With statuesque bearing, a well-presented black suit, and senatorial gray hair, Religious Brother of Mary, Paul Schneider embodied a true foreign-language scholar. Yet he was in truth an adventurer. Brother Paul taught Spanish in a way which elicited not only good students, but enthusiastic admirers.

He kept us spellbound on dreary St. Louis rainy days with tales of his treks through withering, jaguar and fer-de-lance snake infested Peruvian jungles. He explained how he arrived there only after he'd pumped his lungs to bursting marching through Quechua Indian territory. He described to young men who'd never left city streets what it was like to dine in villas with Spanish descendants in coastal Lima, Peru, and later in huts with Quechuas thousands of feet above sea level in the Andes Mountains. He detailed how his Spanish skills got him to Peru, and his language abilities helped him master several Indian dialects thereafter. The Gray Fox was not only a good Spanish teacher, but someone I wanted to be like.

Brother Paul told of meeting men so historically wealthy they traced their forebears to Spanish Conquistadors. One had marble figures of his children carved to line the tree-garlanded road inside his walled and gated compound. Brother Paul discerned also the poor of Peru using these same villa's exterior walls as props for their lean-to cardboard huts and open-air cook pots. He explained how Quechua Indians used coca leaves to numb their hunger and so survive endless Andean journeys at several miles' height above sea level. Each of the Gray Fox's personal stories introduced something new, which he described with a clarity so fine we felt as if we'd been there. He left it up to us to think about what he'd described, and then ask our own questions about what he'd observed. We did this all in Spanish, of course. Thus we found ourselves unwittingly compelled to think and use new words and new thoughts in a foreign language. He described not only a story, but the utility and beauty of words, and their facility in expressing more intense meanings. By this remarkable technique he captured first our interest, then our imagination. After that, he developed our discernment. Indeed, he showed that without prejudging a situation, and reflecting on what we had seen and heard, we could arrive at the truth. We need only listen and see, then patiently reflect upon, and so discern the meaning of what we saw. The magic all took place through a foreign language. To ask deeper questions required deeper thoughts, and so deeper words and sentence construction. I wanted to be like him.

Brother Paul made it clear he'd only gotten to Peru because of his language ability. "You know, John," he said to me one indifferent Missouri day, "If you keep up your language study, it will change your life."

Professor Norris K. Smith

Professor Norris K. Smith of Washington University in St. Louis caused art and architecture to enter my life forever. He introduced and helped me understand, in often astounding ways, those realities of my world. He explained in a consistent doctrine how architecture and artistic renderings challenge the viewer to affirm or deny what is asserted to be true by the builder or artist. This consciousness engaged me my entire life since then. I cannot pass a piece of public art, or building, without recalling what Professor Smith taught me. He made it possible for me to know how to reflect on what underlies the creation of a work of art or a public building, what gives it meaning. How for example, did the Greeks want to represent the role of the citizen when they built the Acropolis, or the Romans their Forum? What did Stalin mean when he built a block-like mammoth building on a place where he'd destroyed the church that once stood there? What did Hitler assert to be true about the new Nazi Germany when he raised the gigantic *Olympiastadion* (1936 Olympic Stadium) in Berlin? How do these and other places inform us today? Do we believe or reject what these buildings' architects attest to be true? What do we affirm or deny about American citizenship when we look at our own ubiquitous, modern, box-like public buildings? Where once our nation made great public art of our capitol, White House, indeed even postal buildings with mighty pillars that recalled Ancient Greece, now we put up square, brick-faced office blocks. Government buildings no longer recall democratic ideals, but rather a flinty financial tight-fistedness which begrudges the very name of public service. Just as Michelangelo's *Pietà* asserts what he believed true about the nature of sacrifice, of loss, from a coherent world view, so Jackson Pollock affirms the absence of such cohesion. When I visited Versailles, I wasn't a casual tourist: I recognized what King Louis XIV believed and attested to be true about himself and his society. At the Coliseum in Rome, my reflection challenged me to think about the fall of an entire society to games and circuses. Indeed, our own Holocaust Museum is built to assert the triumph of mutual understanding over organized racism and death. I can understand all this now.

I can determine my own reaction to these and other assertions thanks to the doctrine and guidance of Professor Smith. Such a gift is immeasurable because it made my entire life fuller.

George came into my life when I saw him sitting at the end of the counter at my first job in an ice cream parlor. He sat there from morning until closing. He never spoke except to order a soda. After a while, he didn't even need to do that.

GEORGE

"Out, George!" Yelled my boss to the man at the end of the counter.

That closing time ritual went on as long as I worked at the ice cream store.

"Who is that guy?" I asked one day.

Every day he'd order a single coke, then sit there, eyes down, saying nothing.

Out of the St. Louis cold, I supposed.

"George? Some guy who lost his brother in the war. Now he wanders the alleys at nights looking for him.

He'll be out there in the daytime too, once the weather gets nice. Guy's crazy."

Some years later I saw George again

Walking in an alley.

Looking for his lost brother to come home.

PART II: WAR, ESPIONAGE, AND TERRORISM

War is sweet to those who haven't experienced it.--Latin Quotation

It is the same in all wars; the soldiers do the fighting, the journalists do the shouting, and no true patriot ever gets near a front-line trench, except on the briefest of propaganda-tours.--George Orwell, **Homage to Catalonia**

Where Did It All Begin?

Armed with little beyond a rudimentary training in counterespionage, basic German, and a European history degree from Washington University in St. Louis, I was deployed to Europe during the Cold War. I had only four years of artillery experience with the 101st Air Assault Division under my belt; that is to say, no counterintelligence experience at all.

The experiences of my European counterintelligence colleagues, some of whom were twenty to twenty-five years older than me, filled in massive gaps in my education. I began to see not only world events, but the impact of such events on real people, all with faces, families, and a personal story. Most of my European colleagues, in fact, had personally survived the Second World War, and saw my world in that context. When I first saw the relentless Iron Curtain at Phillipsthal, a small town in West Germany, I came to believe even more clearly that people should be free to pursue life as they wanted. No relentless ideology strutting around behind a giant Wall should tell them how.

The Iron Curtain of the Cold War was the corner of a lifetime, around which I wanted to peer, if not help bring down. I wanted to discover the truth and understand what was behind all this suspicion, hatred and, above all, fear. Reflecting on my search now, it seems almost childlike in its simplicity. Yet to fashion our lives' works around our hopes is not so childlike, really. I wasn't afraid to try. Fear can paralyze any hope for the future. If we can't imagine anything but bad, or try to find new ways around old, old difficulties, we'll stay locked where we are forever. We'll miss out on what might make our lives, and our children's lives, happier and more intense, broader, and so less fearful.

I was a soldier and civil servant. My life as an Army combat arms officer, then counterintelligence agent, linguist, and student of human nature, brought me and my family many places others have not been. Since I was involved in the secret world of Cold War counterespionage, and that war's bloody aftermath of ethnic violence, religious hatreds, and political terrorism, you'll find I reflect much on our peculiar American appeal to warfare and violence. Why we are like this has always been a mystery to me. Paradox prevails, however, in how we are also among the most hopeful people on earth. Why that is so brought me to reflection on many a long walk on rain-swept nights, watching gray clouds, stars sparkling then vanishing away again, as rain waves passed by. I walked alone in quiet thought, every night, rain or, as Europeans say, no rain.

Perhaps it was my fascination with mystery that drew me to my profession in the secret world after years with artillery and infantrymen. My particular role was as a counterintelligence officer and linguist in the US Army. I was a 'detective' and liaison officer during the Cold War and its kaleidoscopic, not to say chaotic aftermath. We investigated espionage and terrorism directed against our army and allies in Europe. To have any success at all, I found I had to know something of myself, as Socrates advised. To know the others in whose world I walked, I had to learn languages. To do either of these, to learn of myself and foreign cultures and languages, required negotiating the most difficult of 'corners'. Through a discernment of one's faults, and language study, one learns humility, patience, and careful, careful listening. Humility, patience and listening are traits not readily identified with Americans. One learns, as Sherlock Holmes counseled his friend Watson, "They say that genius is an infinite capacity for taking pains," he remarked with a smile. "It's a very bad definition, but it does apply to detective work."

Professionalism grows in such a garden.

So my professional world began during the great standoff between the former Allies of World War II. We found ourselves in the West, and the Soviet Union and its Pact allies beyond their Iron Curtain in the East. It was not a shooting war; rather it featured proxy conflicts, debased secret betrayals, plots, espionage, subversion, and indeed, periodic killings. It was a tenuous peace. Thus violence figured as a gray eminence in every aspect of my life, from crime in American streets, to the grand American containment strategy. The latter brought me and my family to Europe as a consequence. The failures of diplomacy at the end of the Cold War set the stage for more, seemingly intractable violence and terror in the Balkans, the Middle East, and now the world. Slaughter proved an all-too-ready answer for the world's new problems in previously unremarkable places like Srebrenica, Sarajevo, Kabul, Baghdad, and even tiny American towns like Newtown, Connecticut. Too often such violence only bred preliminary causes to serve as preludes for even worse conflicts and violence to come. You'll find my stories don't leave these thoughts in the abstract. I want to show how abstract policies affect real people, with names and families. I want to show how, at least in my life, real people I knew were impacted in hydra-headed ways apparent only upon reflection on these experiences. As you'll see, we who are called upon to fight and understand wars, assess intelligence, and deal with violence in nations or local communities, find they affect us as Americans often in utterly unpredictable ways. We become different when we try to understand ourselves, our predilections, our prejudices. It becomes important to look around the corner, to see and try to understand the other who lives there. Not for nothing did I realize, as I'll show in many of these stories, that my colleagues were stamped with the impact of the Second World War. We learn that every life's role carries significance, regardless of how or when it is played.

THE LOST AMERICAN

I've seen the actual photograph, taken from the wing camera of an American Helldiver bomber. A gray plume of smoke rising from atop a vessel from several hundred feet belies the gust of fire, shrapnel, and death that accompanied the blast. That bursting bomb struck the Japanese ship *Enoura Maru*, carrier of some 1290 American prisoners in medieval conditions of abuse and starvation.

Aboard the ship was an American soldier, a West Point graduate named Donald Richard Snoke. He'd commanded a Coast Artillery battery on Corregidor Island, last defense of the American forces in the Philippines in 1942. Snoke, a Pennsylvanian, graduated from West Point in 1939, just in time for deployment to the Pacific. There Japanese Imperial warships maneuvered and armies marched. The Japanese occupation of Manila was brutal, and their treatment of those who surrendered Homeric in its wickedness and cruelty.

Snoke survived two years of captivity, starvation, and torture. He did so despite a death-rate unmatched in American military history. After almost two years of such trial he, with several hundred others, was taken aboard the *Oryoku Maru*, a so-called 'hell ship'. There his purgatory only continued.

Fighters from the USS Hornet caught the *Oryoku* near dock side, and struck with a vengeance, ironically killing many American prisoners on the unmarked vessel. Once bombed, the desperate prisoners leapt into the sea, trying to swim ashore. The unwitting Allied pilots strafed the water, and the Japanese machine-gunned the men from shore. Mad with thirst and horror, none of the Americans escaped, and were recaptured. Snoke survived, to confront an almost diabolical trick. The surviving prisoners were directed to select their most injured compatriots, so that they could be treated by Japanese doctors. Once selected, the prisoners were simply murdered out of hand by their Japanese captors.

It was aboard another hell ship, the *Enoura Maru*, that Snoke's journey continued. It was to be on that ship when another American bomb ended his pain. It was the photograph I viewed that was the image of the bomb strike that killed him.

You'd think a man who gave the last full measure of devotion would be hallowed in word and deed in our nation. For he did serve, despite every evil visited upon him. What happened to Captain Snoke? His body and those of some three hundred other massacred prisoners were moved to Hawaii after the war, where they were interred in a mass grave. Their names are known, but their bodies are not matched to their family members' DNA samples. This could be done now, but money for such a project has been wasted by the Joint POW/MIA Accounting Command. This command has instead been holding fraudulent 'arrival ceremonies' for years in Hawaii. There, grieving relatives perform unwitting roles as extras in this farce, as they are led to believe their honored dead were returned home in flag-draped caskets. The *Stars and Stripes* newspaper revealed this fraud, indeed showed the aircraft couldn't even fly, and the organizers themselves called the event the 'Big Lie'. It is now time to make it right, after so long, to specifically identify the body of Captain Snoke and his comrades, and return them to their families, our fellow Americans.

*My wife's dad, Duane L. Tedrick, joined Delta Company, 2/506th Parachute Infantry Regiment during World War II. Many have heard of Echo Company of that same regiment, **The Band of Brothers**. Although he retired as a Sergeant Major in the US Army, most of his memories resonated a melancholic appreciation of how the Second World War affected him as a young man. The following several essays are based upon conversations we had together. This strange event happened one winter's night to his squad while they passed through a Belgian field, and stopped in a barn.*

GUARDIAN AT THE GATE

Bone-aching filthy scarecrows with machine guns and carbines kicked open the barn-door. Finding the place empty, they collapsed for the night.

One threw his rolled-up web belt down for a pillow, and claimed the only hay bin in the darkened cow shed. Better to sleep on the box cover's too-short wooden slats than to spend another night like a dog on the freezing ground.

With the pre-dawn, in half-dreaming wakefulness, walking like dead men, the encrusted-eyed GIs moved out, to face another day at war with Germans. One man's Wild Bill Hickok mustache alone stirred a smile, since it survived another night when others thought it would break off with the ice.

Only a couple days later would they hear that hay bin contained wonders beyond imagination. Titians, an El Greco, a couple of Dutch Masters paintings, and smaller treasures were there, rolled up and hidden by some cultural vandal.

For that brief night, the mustached American paratrooper was like the Roman centurion of yore, protecting civilization with his very body.

ENEMIES ON D-DAY

Norman coastal weather is crisp and bracing. Winds and frequent rains appear, diminish and reappear. The sky stays various shades of gray. The beaches consist of tiny stones that mix poorly with sand. This sand abuts steep white rock cliffs topped by thick, ancient vegetation. Where populated, a stone seawall secures the compact towns. The North Sea itself remains cold, even in June.

I visited Normandy with my family. We were there 47 years after my wife's father combat jumped, or more properly, fell into the Norman plain beyond the hard coastline. He fought there on D-Day, the day of the great Allied invasion of Europe. On that same day, in a nearby French village, a German soldier who would years later become our good friend awaited news of the grand assault.

My wife's dad was a team leader of paratroopers. His squad was selected to blow up a bridge on a road leading to the coast. That accomplished, German reinforcements would be hindered in reaching the invasion beaches.

He flew with some 10 other Americans cramped in an olive-green glider. They took off from England on the moonlit night of June 5, 1944. He had a 36-pound demolition charge strapped to his leg for his part of this behind-the-lines mission. After destroying the bridge, they would reunite with their regiment at a drop zone.

German staff officers anticipated such a maneuver. They opened the dikes and levees controlling ancient, drained swamps. Thus they flooded miles of flatlands, that is to say, of potential parachute drop zones. Hundreds of antiaircraft guns in concrete embrasures along the coast covered potential aircraft approach routes.

My sons sat on such an empty anti-aircraft gun emplacement, taking off their socks. They ran down the sea wall and across the beach 200 yards to the ocean waves. There, among the French and English sunbathers, they were unaware of another German defensive measure, visible about 50 meters away. Flush against stone outcroppings were other gun emplacements. These were positioned at either end of the beach to rake oblique machine-gun bursts into the bodies of landing soldiers. I rested against the concrete anti-aircraft gun position fastened to the stone sea-wall. I noted the irony of a place once at war, but where now the children's children of that war's soldiers played, innocent of all its horrors. As I watched the boys chase the waves, I wondered whether this very anti-aircraft gun shot down that glider 47 years ago.

My wife's father remembered the co-pilot, blood blowing across his face from the shell impact that killed the pilot, cry wildly, "We're hit boys, you better jump now!" Everyone scrambled in the dark. With sweaty and clammy skin they heaved their equipment toward the door. A din of shouted fear, anger and encouragement vanished into absolute silence as each man hurled himself out into the black night.

In the distance, gunfire and shellfire laced the sky. Surrounded by darkness, he didn't know whether he was over the sea or the ocean or land. The splash horrified him. His rifle, equipment, parachute and demolition charge dragged him straight down like a modern-day millstone. Only the issued switch-blade knife saved him from drowning. He cut all the straps of the embracing military gear, and rejoiced to burst above the waterline and breathe. He had landed in a flooded plain, surrounded by Norman hedgerows, toward which he swam.

That same night, a regiment of German soldiers in the Ninth Army Division received conflicting orders. They marched to and fro, unsure of where the actual landing would occur. The fog of war was complete. Noise and gunfire erupted everywhere, but in the night sound surrounds the listener, it does not assist. These Germans never reached the landing beaches, and so our friend did not fight on that invasion day. Due to Allied deception, his unit was misdirected to a false landing beach. The Germans only recovered their orientation when it was too late and the Allies were ashore.

The American wandered weaponless for almost two days until he came upon a dead paratrooper, hanging by his parachute in a tree. The German soldier, for his part, was among the last to evacuate Rouen, France, after the battle of Normandy was over. He ruefully remembered watching German V-1 "buzz bombs" slam into Rouen.

He said, "We weren't even over the bridge and our own rockets were fired at us. Whole blocks disintegrated into dust as the rockets struck. The rockets were supposed to blow up the bridges over the Seine, but we were known to still be on the other side. I later learned that we were indeed the intended targets! Hitler never forgave us for retreating. He had ordered us to die at the landing beaches and resist the Allies to the last bullet and man. We were forbidden to retreat."

I'm glad these two men did not come across the each other in those deadly days. One is my father-in-law; the other is one of our good friends and the father of other friends. I'm happy that by some strange alchemy reconciliation occurred between my American family and our German friends.

I often wonder if these two men had met under other circumstances, if they might not have been good friends, too. The wry World War I saloon refrain seems even more poignant when I think of it in this context:

> *We might have met at a barstool,*
> *Or waved from passing trains,*
> *Instead we met on Flanders Fields,*
> *And I blew out your brains.*

MARKET GARDEN

Thousands upon thousands of young American men bounded from aircraft over the Netherlands some seventy plus years ago. This was part of the grand assault on Nazi-held territory known as Operation Market Garden. One was my father in law, then Corporal Duane L. Tedrick, D Company, 2nd Battalion, 506th Parachute Infantry Regiment. They landed in flat fields, crisscrossed by canals, which stretched as far as the eye could see. He was a member of the 101st Airborne Division, and his job was to help take bridges near the town of Eindhoven.

They were warned before the great battle to avoid contact with adult Dutch Resistance personnel. The word was that they had been compromised by the Germans. How this had happened, no one knew. No one knew at the time that German counterintelligence had captured and 'turned' many spies sent from England to report to London. No one knew that one of the primary Dutch resistance men had been 'turned' in return for his brother's life. No, no one knew any of this, though it was suspected.

My wife Jane's dad met young Dutch people, who came up to his little squad. He showed them his map and asked, "Waar zijn de Duitsers?" His anglicized version of "Where are the Germans" was readily answered. The Dutch resisters pointed to all points of the compass on his map. They were everywhere, he recalled, "We were surrounded!" His battle only lasted another day, until he was wounded by a mortar blast. Sent after the battle to England, he recovered in time for the Battle of the Bulge.

They Fought for Us All

Belgium is virtually always overcast. The Ardennes Forest is dense with evergreen pines, which trick the eye toward twilight when they appear black. A gloomy fog coats the riverbeds each morning and is slow to lift because the sun seldom penetrates the gray shroud of sky. This is a dark land where belief in mysterious legends is common. This is what Allied troops faced so many winters ago. November 1944 brought perhaps the worst rains in memory to the Ardennes. The few roads through it were sucking bogs of mud.

In 47 years, little had changed. My family and I went to Bastogne to visit the place where my wife's father, Sgt. Duane L. Tedrick, once fought in the titanic Battle of the Bulge. Few markers indicate where, under heavy clouds, about a quarter of a million German soldiers in their armored columns secretly assembled. Modern German highways skirt the once-famous Siegfried Line. This is an actual physical line in the fields composed of thousands upon thousands of tremendous concrete blocks. These blocks stand six across and stretch for hundreds of kilometers. They mark the old western German frontier and were meant to stop tanks. In places, one can walk among these "dragon's teeth." Behind this barrier, named for the mythic King Siegfried, Adolf Hitler planned a counteroffensive designed to overwhelm the Americans and drive the Allies toward the sea. Weirdly, his plan to strike in the third great winter since the invasion of Russia corresponded with the decisive third winter of war foretold in the legend of the Twilight of the Gods.

Winter came viciously that year. It was so terrible that those who looked for omens could not but be astonished at the good fortune that befell the Germans. Just as in the legend, the Teutonic heroes could arise to a conquering horn calling forth the furor of the Germanic folk. The Germans were hidden from the Allies' superior air force by whirling rains, winds and snow. In such weather, the German legions swept through the forest. The terror of surprise caused an early rout of the Americans, who surrendered or fled to the rear, offering little resistance, Gen. Dwight D. Eisenhower prepared to plug the widening gap with human clay. He called upon the 101st Airborne Division as one of the reserve elements to stop the Germans. My wife's father recalls the flurry of events as the paratroopers were trucked in and then marched to the front. Upon arrival, they spread out around the cross-roads town of Bastogne.

The very place where his unit, the 2/506th Parachute Infantry Regiment, dug in is even today a pine forest. Vaguely recognizable depressions mark where our American ancestors prepared to meet the onslaught. It is hard to imagine now the pure panic of those days. Where today only the occasional squirrel watches, Americans fled for their lives, were shot down or were obliterated by the terrible German 88 mm artillery pieces. The driven, retreating Americans who remained were rounded up by the paratroopers and formed into haphazard units. The intensifying snow finally slowed the Germans too, but by then the airborne soldiers were surrounded in Bastogne.

The weather deteriorated. Men watched one another for signs of frostbite. My father-in-law fell dead asleep during a break in the nearly constant fighting, and it almost proved to be fatal. When a comrade woke him, he could no longer feel his feet. His first fear was frostbite and he became desperate. A horse, covered with lesions and therefore inedible, wandered through the area. With a .45-caliber pistol, he shot it, then slit its belly and thrust his feet into the hot stomach. A searing pain finally hit him, and he knew he had saved himself from the horrors of frostbite.

Similar desperate measures were taken by other Americans long ago at Valley Forge.

To a squad leader like my father-in-law, the grand tactics meant nothing. His men were to dig in, watch a bit of forest and kill any German who came their way. And so they did, killing and digging, on and on, over and over. The intensity of a life that could instantly end focused their attention on every sound they heard. He recalls a particularly haunting incident that occurred shortly before Christmas 1944. Toward evening, far off in the forest, a German loudspeaker began to play American Christmas carols. Across the silent white snow, through the black trees and under the winter moon came the eerie sound of Bing Crosby's "White Christmas."

The surreal music was made even more sinister when a German, speaking perfect English, said, "Good evening, American paratroopers. Don't you wish you were home now? Listen. On our Christmas menu we'll be having turkey with gravy and stuffing. Of course there will be fresh vegetables, too. Oh yes, and for you Southern boys there will be plenty of baked ham and grits on the side."

This, said to a man in a frozen hole eating another K ration after days of siege, was almost unbearable. "All you have to do, Americans," the German continued, "is to walk 300 meters in our direction with your hands up, and then you can join us for the Christmas feast."

The G.I.s didn't, of course. They held on. Despite their lack of winter uniforms, the lack of armored protection and the constant killing and maiming of those they had lived beside for three years, they held on. Later they learned that they were considered the heroes of Bastogne, who withstood the German Blitzkrieg in the Battle of the Bulge.

A few days later, Sergeant D.L. Tedrick was blasted by a German Tiger tank shell. He was found incoherently dragging his Browning automatic rifle by the barrel as he wandered aimlessly on a path through Noville, Belgium. He survived. Before the end of January, the Allies had triumphed.

As I leaned against the hood of my car on a Belgian forest track, I tried to imagine the heroism displayed at that place by our forefathers so very long ago. Real soldiers never speak of their heroism. Few realize it even when acting it out. Did they later realize the sacrifice they offered for those of us yet to be born? What we are today has meaning only in light of the past. What our ancestors fought for has shaped our lives.

Life isn't relative. Some things are worth fighting for.

RESISTANCE CAVE

My family and I stopped at a *trattoria* in the verdant springtime countryside of northern Italy in the mid 1980's. *Trattorias* are a typically imaginative Italian restaurant such as we have not yet invented in America. What's special is you can enjoy a wonderful dinner, prepared only with regional foods and wines, with the very local people who grew them. In these one-of-a-kind places you'll find not only area delights, but often vegetables or animals raised by the owner himself, not to mention his wine! Especially beloved in a country that loves children, the kids can play outside in the *trattoria* yard while mom and dad talk away at the long common tables. At one such place, we discovered this remarkable story.

The owner was glad my barely passable Italian was available, because he wanted to tell me something. "You are the first English speaker here since the war!"

"Really," I answered. "Were they also Americans?"

"No, they were Englishmen," he exclaimed, his every word punctuated with appropriate, elaborate, operatic hand and eye gestures. "In fact, we saw their plane get hit and glide down pulsing a cloud of smoke. Then we saw a 'pop' when the pilots' parachutes opened. They floated down like snowflakes as their airplane crashed behind the hills. He pointed to the crest of a ridge-line above the town. "Several of us went up into the hills, and we found two of them. They were scared, and one had a broken leg. This was bad."

"Did you hide them then? How long were they here?"

"We took them up to the cave, where a doctor could look at them and the fascists wouldn't know. Hey!" He exulted, "Why don't we go see the cave!" I thought I understood him, and said, "Sure. Let's go!" And then to the boys I advised we were off on another 'mighty adventure.' My wife Jane intervened to say she'd keep Kenny, our youngest, by her, since we were going to do some 'rock climbing.'

I found out the old man wasn't joking, and we did do some rock climbing. We followed a picturesque creek that fed into the stream by the restaurant. The weeds and brambles became denser, and as we walked our gait became angular while the trees became thicker. Finally, drenched in sweat, the old *trattoria* owner said, "Now we climb!" The old man appeared to have his fifteen-year-old eyes from when he did this during the war, but luckily for me, he now had a sixty-ish body. We clambered up vines and rocks on the perpendicular cliff face, until at last we came to a man-sized slice into the side of the mountain. It really was there, a cave where the resistance brought those they would hide, and those who were wounded. As we climbed in he showed us the places where smoke had lit the caves, then where they'd run wires and ropes to hold equipment and people.

Our remarkable day over, we climbed down, swearing eternal friendship between Italy, America, and England. "We wanted to fight the fascists. I'm so glad you saw our cave!"

I'll never forget that day. Looking around at those farmers in that well-kept Italian riverine district, I tried to imagine what the Nazis thought of these people when they first came through. Did they consider them inferior people to be pushed around? Or did they remember these people's ancient Roman ancestors produced one of the greatest civilizations on earth?

He wouldn't let us pay for anything, either.

My Hero

He will never plan an ambush.
He'll never call in napalm.
He will never memorize the five paragraph field order.
Nor will he ever hurt anyone.
He won't know malice, or hatred, or envy;
For he will be forever eight years old.
And at sixty four will still enjoy the outdoors, playing catch with a cousin,
And helping to carry in groceries, like he did when his 'mommy' was alive.
He will only cry when someone he loves goes away, or dies,
Or when a bird can't fly, or dog can't play anymore.
He will only know love, and what it means to be kind.

In my career, many of my European colleagues and friends were much older than I. They'd experienced World War II, and in many a conversation offered observations which enlightened this essay.

RESISTANCE OR TERRORISTS?

It was a day-to-day battle with the Gestapo, the Quislings, and the Japanese Secret Police, one long continuous struggle, with torture and unbelievable suffering and death waiting around every corner at every moment.
      Sir Colin Gubbins, Chief, Special Operations Executive, SOE.

Europe was a vast Nazi prison. Into each conquered nation, the Hitler government sent a huge bureaucracy. This bureaucracy existed to suppress the beaten populations, to make them subservient to their new German masters. To do so, it began not with mass torture and killing, although that had featured greatly in the physical conquest of these nations. No, its role was to identify, tabulate, monitor, and control entire populations, their movements, their needs, and their property.

The Germans had many assistants. Natives of the conquered populations were often willing to help. Some helped because they believed Nazi Germany was a bulwark against Soviet Communism, others because they felt there was no other choice, yet others because they only wanted to survive. They did so for their continued employment, for their family, or for money. In any case, the Germans were not alone in administering their triumph. They could also rely on the passive acquiescence of the conquered peoples to supply their endless demands for census records, food depositories, utility schematics, and a host of other records, documents, and files that controlled civilian life.

In time, new, more stringent controls of every sort were introduced. A proper census identified who was where, down to the number of people in each house. A listing of people by race and type was implemented. Soon, Jewish people were identified with a badge of a six-pointed yellow star, which they were required to wear above the waist at all times. Age and gender groups were identified. As the war dragged on, a great manpower shortage in the German war industries led to all the conquered lands being forced to provide labor, and this comprehensive recording system helped the occupation authorities find workers. People received food coupons only if they were registered with the bureaucracy.

Of course, some objected to these measures. Labor strikes, as in the Netherlands, were often violently suppressed with arrests of leaders, who were then interned in the new horror, the concentration camp. German euthanasia policy caused Catholic bishops, during their sermons, to lead their people in protest. This was met with mass arrests of priests and deportation of Jewish converts. To limit the opposition's ability to communicate, the Nazis ensured that all printing presses, typewriters and even paper were registered or surrendered to the government. Since popular communication of the day was by radio, radio sets also had to be registered or turned in. In general, only receivers set to German official government channels were allowed. Movement was controlled. Administrative passes issued by police headquarters alone authorized travel throughout a district. Most effective was the control of food and supplies. Every single person had to be registered in order to eat, and what he could eat was limited by a card in his name identifying food by weight, or supplies by measurement. Indeed, the first primitive computer was employed, ominously, to register Jewish people.

To ensure this system worked, the use of informants rewarded with money, or food, or other benefits, was common. When the threat of loss of a job, or of food, or property didn't stop resistance to the New German Order, jail and even death were proclaimed as official penalties.

The rule of law changed. Government in occupied countries slowly ceased to be a matter of laws, becoming instead one by decrees by military rulers. The means of legally challenging these decrees ceased to exist. It became less and less possible to know what the law was, as it could change overnight. Dread fell over the land. People could be snatched off the street for labor, as hostages, or for no reason at all. Fears of what happened in mysterious concentration camps, where prisoners were detained without indictment or trial, spread throughout the conquered lands. All of this was intended to keep populations in fear, and under control.

From the day Hitler and Stalin invaded and divided Poland between themselves, no power seemed capable of holding back the Nazi tide. Against this continental collapse, only the British government still stood firm against the Nazi march.

Winston Churchill, the new British Prime Minister, faced with his army driven from the European mainland, decided upon a bold initiative. He would strike the Germans unawares. He devised the Special Operations Executive, the SOE, which would create a new front behind the German lines from which to fight Hitler!

The SOE was given the mission "to set Europe ablaze." But how? What would be the specific missions of such an organization? It was determined that the missions for SOE would be very specific. First, it would assist in the rescue of downed pilots, or European soldiers who wanted to continue the fight against Hitler, and help them to secretly travel to Britain to join the fight again. This mission was not primary, however, since it was well established already by other British organizations.

Secondly, it would provide reports of German troop movements, supply depots, and military locations, as well as any plans to invade England.

Thirdly, it would report on weapons developments, local conditions, and changes to military units and plans. This would allow the allies to plan for their promised invasion to come. To report this intelligence would require SOE agents to know radio procedure and code work to transmit such information to London.

Fourthly, it would cause subversion and sabotage. First SOE would identify those who wanted to fight against the Nazi occupation forces, and then organize and train them. The intent in the early part of the war was to tie down German forces protecting rear areas, but not to bring about a national uprising. On D-Day, the goal was to have targeted, local uprisings to support simultaneous military efforts. Essentially untrained civilians were not to rise up alone.

Lastly, SOE would train and supply these groups to prepare for, and then fight the guerrilla battle against the Nazi occupying army. It was this last theme which set the SOE mission apart. Non- uniformed fighters would be SOE-trained in sabotage, attack, and assassination, the better to strike at the hated Nazi army, but only when the time was right. Too early, and the resistance elements could be destroyed, and their value lost. The time had to be just right, but when was that?

 Note as well that there was no mention of assisting Jewish people to escape the Nazi threat. At this time no one knew of the plans of the Nazi 'Final Solution of the Jewish Problem', the mass murder of Jewish people.

Initially, it had to be decided who would best serve in such a unit as SOE? Were they, after all, to be an army unit? A person dropped behind German lines and captured in civilian clothing would be immediately identified as a spy, unprotected by the Hague Conventions, and thus eligible to be executed. So, all SOE persons would be in one form or fashion enrolled in a military unit in the hope that if captured, they would be treated properly as prisoners of war. This, regrettably, did not help. German authorities considered anyone captured behind the lines, even service personnel in uniform, to be terrorists. Once captured, most SOE persons were executed after interrogation and torture, or sent to concentration camps. There most died of exposure, starvation, or were executed by specific order later in the war.

It was decided that SOE should be formed of men and women who were proficient in the language of the targeted European country, were physically fit, and able to blend into any sort of environment. They could thus pretend to be simple Europeans going about their daily jobs. The source for such team members was first the British or Commonwealth armed forces. There were many officers who had grown up in Europe, spoke several languages, and were already available for action. Next there was the need for women agents. Men in occupied Europe were always suspected. Their papers were carefully checked because they could be eligible for forced labor, escaped prisoners, or resistance fighters hidden in the 'underground'. Women became particularly valuable in the secret war because they were believed, in that day, to be relatively innocent, and less likely to be engaged in secret work. Their movements were not as rigidly controlled. This was to SOE's great advantage.

SOE had learned that early, small, independent European resistance organizations were quickly rolled up by the Gestapo. This is because they operated on personal lines and had almost no clandestine skills. Most of them knew all the underground fighters in their groups through friendship, family, or in a proper chain of command. Once captured, these early resistance personnel were subjected to any number of Gestapo tactics, from kindness, to blackmail, to appeals to military protocol, to horrific tortures. Then, the resistance person would tell all he knew, and the entire organization would be destroyed. Interestingly, the only group that was initially impervious to this was the secret Communist underground. They had years of experience in conducting secret operations in close-knit five-person cells, for they had been outlawed for years by the governments they were trying to subvert before the war started. In these small groups, the capture of one member might only mean the loss of up to five people, since only one person had a contact in the next cell. So it was that many of the best early resistance fighters against the Nazis were Communists, whose aid the liberal democratic government of the United Kingdom welcomed, so long as they fought against Hitler.

Once captured, the resistance people were interrogated by the secret services of the German military or the Gestapo. What information they revealed was collected for further so-called 'counter- terrorist' actions. When finished with their interrogations, these early prisoners were then either turned against their former employers, executed, or sent to concentration camps in Germany. There was virtually no law under which the German secret services operated, save that of effectiveness.

This sinister world is what confronted the new SOE, whose headquarters, ironically, was on Baker Street, in London, the same street as the imaginary office of Sherlock Holmes. They set about gathering people for the mission. Their training corresponded to what was known of the brutal German 'counterterrorist' tactics in Europe. In time, not only resistance fighters, but even commandos in uniform were subject to immediate execution. Even more hideous, the Night and Fog decree stated that anyone so captured would be sent into Night and Fog, never to be heard from again.

Training for the quietly, individually recruited SOE personnel was done in the British countryside, often on the grounds of grand old stately aristocratic houses. First, they were given physical training, because their life, once in Europe, would be demanding. For instance, since telephones and telegraphs were considered compromised and monitored by German counterintelligence, many messages were delivered by foot or by bicycle, over dozens of miles every day. SOE personnel were taught Morse code, for that was how messages were to be relayed back to British headquarters in London. Such messages were sent via wireless transmitters that were for their day compact, the size of a large briefcase. Most often, the location of the radio was moved after the transmission. Agents were never to deliver transmitters in person; someone else would do so. This way, a person delivering a radio who was caught, but did not know the code, could not reveal even under torture how it sent messages. Most of the women initially sent to Europe were wireless telegraph operators, because these devices required an operator who could travel with relative ease to wherever the next radio location would be.

SOE members were trained as well in the organization of 'drop areas', since supplies for resistance personnel were brought in by aircraft which would either land or drop their cargo by parachute. Such aircraft would approach the European coast on moonlit nights, flying low, under the newly-developed German radar. They would fly until they found lights, either provided by bonfires, headlights, or flashlights, and then drop their cargoes of weapons and personnel. To this end, all candidates for SOE work were trained in parachuting skills. Of course, once on the ground, they were linked up with resistance organizations, if there were any. Trainees also learned close combat as well as firearms expertise. Most significant, they were trained how to blow things up. Their skills with explosives were to be their great contribution to the war effort. They would train the locals on how to perform sabotage. Indeed, the well-trained saboteur was often better at precision targeting than Allied bomber raids!

The question all must answer is: what were the targets? When should they be hit? In short, how were these various SOE teams organized for action? New officers, for even the women were usually commissioned as officers, would arrive with specific missions to organize locals. These SOE circuits were then responsible for given geographical areas. They would identify people ready to act, train them, and gather information. Mission updates, requests for supplies, or vital information would be sent via radio transmitter to London, and further guidance received. Great danger arose every time a transmitter was used. German direction-finding devices were very advanced, and could triangulate on transmissions in minutes. This was the greatest threat to resistance operatives. Communication by this means was therefore only for actual emergencies, to organize supply drops, and to advise of critical needs or changes. More often, London would communicate via the British Broadcasting Corporation's strange nightly 'personal messages', known only to resistance teams. Sent at a certain hour of the night, these messages were relatively easy to receive throughout the continent. "Veronique expects her kittens to be cared for." "Thomas collects poppies with ease." "Two angels are dancing." These nonsense sentences had meaning only to resistance fighters, and caused actions, or inactions, to occur. Not for nothing was it a punishable offense to listen to foreign broadcasts in Nazi Europe!

And so, nightly drops of military supplies to be used in training, for practice, and for use began throughout Europe. You'll notice that there was no political training for these operatives. Their object was to defeat Hitler, not to engage in European conflicts between communists and non-communist resistance organizations. If in the opinion of the SOE officer the resistance group was willing to fight, they got what they needed from London. If instead the local resistance used the supplies on the black market, or kept the weapons for intended post-war use against their political adversaries, or sat on them, they were cut off. Money was also carefully handled and distributed, as money often bought freedom for prisoners and black-market food for those living unregistered in the underground with bogus identities.

Of course, to oppose these activities, the Germans employed a panoply of counterintelligence methods. They tried to infiltrate resistance circuits. Using English speakers, they would pretend to be downed pilots trying to reach an escape line. To defend against this, SOE devised a way that secret route guides or homeowners at rest stations could check, via radio to London, whether these alleged 'downed pilots' were real.

The Germans also employed secret informers. Resistance prisoners who had been captured and 'turned' were assigned upon their release to report on resistance activities. Torture and fear played a great role here. Simple offers of cash payments attracted and employed others. Often Germans employed their own professionals, such as Sergeant Otto Bleicher. His ability to play various roles in numerous languages was essential to the capture of many resistance personnel. Some informants were blackmailed, and reported in order to keep their families or their jobs safe. Or they did it out of political belief, for many Europeans saw the German Army as the last defense against Soviet Bolshevism. SOE circuits would identify such traitors, and allow their identity to be spread around. News was spread via the BBC and through resistance channels that employed secret newspapers, published by clandestine printing presses or in England. These papers would then be slipped under doorways by young children at night. Not for nothing did the Germans impose a curfew!

Of course, control of retaliation by the resistance against their Nazi tormentors was the hardest form of discipline SOE had to employ. Gestapo agents, traitors, secret police informers, and notoriously efficient government officials were targets crying out to be shot. Yet the Germans' reprisals against attacks on their fellow Germans were horrific. In Poland, an attack against the Gestapo chief of Krakow resulted in the mass execution of innocent people. In Czechoslovakia, the assassination of Deputy Reich Protector Reinhard Heydrich resulted in the massacre of all males aged over 16 in the Czech villages of Lidice and Ležáky, the deportation of all the local women and children to concentration camps, and the murder of hundreds of other prisoners. Generally, it was ten hostages for every German killed, while in Yugoslavia that number rose to two hundred to one toward war's end. German retaliation against the families of identified prisoners and resistance personnel was common.

Oddly, however, executions of local government officials, say a Dutch collaborator by a Dutch patriot, were often handled as police crimes, and investigated as such. This was done to maintain the illusion that an occupied country had control of its own affairs. Of course, the more disciplined the resistance organization, the less random the actions taken and so more planned, targeted actions were possible. For example, in certain towns, the Dutch burned all the personnel records, to make it easier for wanted persons to escape recognition. They stole stamps to allow forgeries to be made and jumbled records to make the Germans lose track of people who were eligible for forced labor. German countermeasures were immediately employed whenever an action took place. They would randomly change the type and registration requirements for identity cards. New types of ration cards, travel authorizations, or of equipment permission requirements and signatures were constantly introduced. This was to trip up SOE efforts to introduce new agents complete with valid identity papers. Of course, when new papers were introduced, SOE agents in the country could communicate this information to London immediately. Forgers, recently released from British prisons, were then set to work making new copies and signatures for the SOE! When all else failed, the British Royal Air Force would drop thousands of newly-made ration cards all over the occupied country, the better to disrupt the Nazi economy measures.

The Nazis were not without their regular victories, however. One notable Allied disaster was Germany's Operation Nordpol. German counterintelligence had succeeded in capturing a Dutch SOE radio operator dropped early in the war. He was convinced to transmit back to his headquarters in London that he had arrived well and was ready to operate. He did so, and later directed further drops of SOE personnel. Each was arrested upon landing in the Netherlands, and their missions compromised. Of course, tragically, each one reported that he had arrived well and secure. One by one, new SOE men were dropped into Holland, only to be captured immediately. Each in turn was coerced by the Germans into working for them. In all, fifty-four Dutch SOE personnel were captured before the so-called "England Spiel" or England Game was uncovered. This only happened when two Allied prisoners escaped to warn London of the disaster. And even then they were not immediately believed, for fear they were spreading disinformation. Whole books have been devoted to why London did not acknowledge the warning messages sent by captured SOE wireless operators in their transmissions. By this means, the agent would send a message with a deliberate error at a specific place to warn of danger. Modern students of this subject ascribe the failure of London to recognize this warning primarily to poor tradecraft, which was only then being developed. Indeed, once identified, the SOE corrected this by giving radio operators a give-away and a genuine warning message. The first could be revealed to the Germans should the wireless person be captured, and the second actually employed if he or she was forced to transmit for the Nazis. Of course, the message transmitted from London which advised one SOE agent, "Don't forget your real warning code!" did not help the war effort.

Sabotage became the primary mission of the SOE once the Allies had decided they were to land on D-Day. All the years of providing intelligence on the size of beaches at high tide, as well as the locations of German armored units, gasoline supply dumps, senior German officers, and thousands of other details were at last put to use. Now, the training of the French Maquis, the armed resistance teams, could be set loose, if only in the areas of actual simultaneous military combat. Just as the SOE teams had already discovered in Italy, these French resistance fighters were more than ready to strike back at their tormentors. They had to be controlled in their responses, lest they be slaughtered without any help from arriving Allied military forces.

And strike with weapons and sabotage they did! It is believed that the trains, railroad tunnels, bridges, telephone poles, electricity units, and viaducts destroyed by the SOE-trained French Resistance kept the powerful "Das Reich" German armored column from arriving in time to drive the Allies off the beaches of Normandy on D-Day. Well-placed bombs exploded in locomotive housing buildings, rail yards, airfields, and factories across embattled France. Some sustain that because they were specifically located, these resistance explosives were more efficient than even strategic bombing. The Allied landings were supported by a massive outpouring of SOE-trained armed resistance behind the German lines. In fact, the urge to strike back was so powerful that General Eisenhower, in command of the invasion, dropped a message to Dutch resistance which cautioned them that although the hour of liberation was at hand, to wait, employ discipline, and not act before the Allies moved into the Netherlands. Ike did not want to risk Nazi reprisals against the Dutch population for no reason.

The price paid by SOE to accomplish its missions was terrible. Fully one quarter of their agents sent to France were killed. Dutch SOE personnel were killed by the score. The horrors they were subjected to by their German captors is well known. Yet studies of the accomplishments of SOE led to many new initiatives in the secret world. Much of what was learned then has kept operatives alive today. These people fought, quite literally, for freedom.

JUST ONE FORGET-ME-NOT

A visitor to Huntsville, Alabama, might think that Wernher von Braun was our favorite son. The huge downtown Civic Center bears his name. The largest building complex on Redstone Arsenal is named after him. Wernher von Braun is lauded and exalted everywhere because he brought America to the moon. America went to the moon on his science. We forgive him the fact that in pursuit of his dream some 20,000 slave laborers and allied civilians gave their lives.

As his research and testing of the German V-1 (buzz bomb) and V-2 rockets progressed, first at Peenemünde, Germany, then in the tunnels of the Dora-Mittelbau concentration camp, thousands died. He was given access to a steady stream of Nazi incarcerated prison labor. These were resistance fighters, Jews, religious opponents, and other dissidents who could be worked until they died building the *Vergeltung* (Revenge) rockets that Hitler wanted. These unprecedented flying bombs were Hitler's secret weapons. Finally, they were fired at Antwerp, at Liège, and of course at London and British targets to try to stop the Allied advance across Europe. Thousands more civilians were blasted to bits as a result of his new technology. When these new mass slaughters failed to halt the Allied push into Germany, World War II came to an end.

We all know the refrain, well, war is war. Everyone had to do his bit. Who hasn't heard that? Of course, that is usually said about soldiers who stand and fight. Seldom is it applied to technicians who fire rockets which can't be defended against, built by slaves who have no names, whose lives mean nothing. The slaves were work-things, disposable. And when they objected, they'd be hung over the main tunnel entrance at Dora-Mittelbau with sticks jammed in their mouths so they couldn't shout out in their dying gasps.

We took the Revenge Rocket technology and refined it. It carried us to the moon. This is among the greatest achievements of our human race. Perhaps we could remember all those who brought us to this pinnacle of science. Why not one forget-me-not, on a discreet stand, perhaps in the Huntsville Botanical Garden, commemorating the dead slaves who helped Mr. von Braun and his colleagues ultimately bring us to the moon? It is only fair.

COFFEE BREAK VISIT

Fulton, Missouri, is nestled in the bounteous center of Missouri. Fulton's small Westminster College, replete with a liberal arts academic atmosphere, encouraging foliage on its vine-wrapped Victorian buildings, and meadow-like campus is a centerpiece of this Midwestern idyll. To this College an English church, one of Sir Christopher Wren's actual masterpieces, was transported from London, stone by registered stone. It was done on the twentieth anniversary of perhaps one of the most significant speeches of all time, by Winston Churchill, the former Prime Minister of Great Britain. It was to visit this campus that my family and I detoured, after my assignment as an artillery officer at Fort Campbell, Kentucky ended. We were enroute to my German language course, set to begin at the Defense Language Institute, in Monterey, California. This chance visit to Westminster would prepare me for my future in a way I could but only imagine.

As guest of President Harry S. Truman in 1946, Mr. Churchill, who'd been out of office for only a few months, spoke on "The Sinews of Peace." In a speech given at this very college campus, Churchill spoke with hope for the future of a war-ravaged Europe. He speculated about a truly empowered United Nations which could stand up against any future threat to the world's tranquility. He believed such a common enterprise could prevent another war; despite his fear that, "from Stettin in the Baltic to Trieste in the Adriatic, an iron curtain has descended across the Continent." Westminster saw the first use of the expression, Iron Curtain.

In the year immediately after the vicious mass slaughter that was World War II, the Allies of that war approached a nadir in their relationships. Churchill was most distraught that Soviet Marshal Stalin, his never quite trusted, or trusting, ally. Stalin seemed engaged in the imposition of Soviet control over all the countries in Eastern and Central Europe his armies had conquered. Where the Red Army stood, or Communist control held sway, those borders hardened to a militarized frontier where democracy ended, and tyranny began. In those lands under Soviet influence beyond this Iron Curtain democracy was never to survive. Churchill lamented that small Communist parties there exercised control far beyond their numbers, all backed by a mammoth Red Army which would not go home.

Yet Churchill hoped that a new United Nations, unlike the doomed League of Nations which had arisen from the First World War, would succeed this time. What propelled his faith in this institution; what could suggest that peace would prevail this time? He postulated that an armed, mutually supported United Nations with rotating military contributions of land, sea, and air forces, would be sufficient to stop any future aggression such as Europe and Asia had suffered during the 1930s. He hoped that now, amid the ruins of an entire world, a common humanity, confronted with starving and suffering millions could at last work hand in hand to end fear, hunger, disease and war forever.

"I speak particularly of the myriad cottage or apartment homes where the wage-earner strives amid the accidents and difficulties of life to guard his wife and children from privation and bring the family up in the fear of the Lord, or upon ethical conceptions which often play their potent part. To give security to these countless homes, they must be shielded from the two giant marauders, war and tyranny. We all know the frightful disturbances in which the ordinary family is plunged when the curse of war swoops down upon the bread-winner and those for whom he works and contrives."

A robust, powerful United Nations, ready to defend commonly held beliefs, could alone defend against the rebirth of tyranny, no matter what ideology lay at its origin. Churchill directly accused the police states, which seemed to blossom behind the Iron Curtain.

"In these States control is enforced upon the common people by various kinds of all-embracing police governments. The power of the State is exercised without restraint, either by dictators or by compact oligarchies operating through a privileged party and a political police. It is not our duty at this time when difficulties are so numerous to interfere forcibly in the internal affairs of countries which we have not conquered in war. But we must never cease to proclaim in fearless tones the great principles of freedom and the rights of man...which through Magna Carta, the Bill of Rights, the Habeas Corpus, trial by jury, and the English common law find their most famous expression in the American Declaration of Independence."

I'm often astounded to see how messages such as this, unexpectedly discovered during a visit to an obscure mid-western campus on my way elsewhere, changed my life. It came unsolicited, but was superbly appropriate to what I was to do. What better way to understand my future in Cold War Europe than to understand that our mission was to defend these great values, with like-minded Allies, against tyranny?

Wars of the future may be avoided when we show possible tyrants that a nation prospers in every way with rights such as these. Tyrannical states or movements may be stayed if they believe we will defend, by allied force if necessary, these rights we have developed through long, hard years of struggle. Indeed, we need others to see us practice what we preach; that we're all in this together; that others need not then fear us, but work equally with us. As a philosopher once said, evil men are always surprised to see that good men can be brave and clever, too.

A Bosnian Story

After my first assignment as an artillery officer with the 101st Air Assault Division, I went to study German at the Defense Language School in Monterey, California in 1979. One of my teachers, a large, blond, one-armed man, had also been an artillery officer. He had served in 1941, in the German *Wehrmacht*. One rainy afternoon he told this story about his experience in Bosnia during World War II.

"I was a captain, an artillery battery commander. We were moving on twisting mountain roads through Yugoslavia, long after their government had capitulated. I was in the lead vehicle, ahead of my men and guns. We drove down one rain-swept forested valley on a single lane road. Except for the falling rain, it seemed so quiet. I remember how quiet it was. Then a tremendous explosion hurled my vehicle completely in the air. When it landed, my driver was dead and my arm was broken. Then the ambush began. From every tree they fired on us! They were not to be seen! Bullets everywhere! My broken arm was hit and hit again. I took my good arm, drew my pistol, and emptied my Luger at the Slavs.

In time we were rescued by reinforcements. But can you imagine! They wore no uniforms! They were of all ages, men, women, and even young ones! I tell you, they didn't fight fair."

A fair fight? The entire, well-armed, well-fed, ruthless German Army was, in time, driven out of the valleys and trails of Yugoslavia. Sir Fitzroy Maclean, then British Liaison Officer to the Yugoslav resistance, commented that one could discover, running like a golden thread through the history of the Yugoslav peoples, a significant tradition that "again and again in their history had served to extricate them from every sort of entanglement." They wanted to be free of others in their own land. The German legions were beaten by poorly armed, embattled country folk. The German might was driven away by "men, women, and even young ones," who would not give up, who were fighting for their land.

Thinking back on that chilly, damp California day as I listened to his story I wonder, is another war something we want? Why? Do we expect a fair fight?

POLICE RETIREMENT

Reflection on a German colleague's father, who served as a police officer in the Rhineland from 1894 to 1933. He was forced into retirement the month the Nazis came to power.

By all accounts he was a fine policeman,
    Then a criminal investigator, imaginative, and thorough.

He could develop and run down leads like no one else,
and captured many, many law breakers.

Together with his fellow officers, he served all his community's people,
    keeping them safe and protected.

His uncanny wisdom he shared with others, and with his promotions helped
    make others as good as he.

His son was most proud of the magnificent enameled award his father received
    when he stood security in Darmstadt for the visiting Tsar of all the Russians.

Now the well-wrought award rested, unremarked, in a dusty, normally closed, cabinet.

It lay next to a later, equally impressive medal which bore a swastika superimposed on a cross,
    which commemorated his retirement from the police in the first months of the Nazi New World Order.

The new masters of the Master Race were glad to be rid of him,
    a throw-back to non- ideological times.

'Give him a bauble and pension him off,
he doesn't understand a thing about criminals.'

SAVING WHOEVER WE CAN

The Jew is not a human being..--Walter Buch, Nazi Senior Judge

*Human dignity consists in the fact that we are a single great family...
the human race. That is the Church's position, that is the true racism.*--
Papal condemnation of racism, L'Osservatore Romano, July, 1937

*The Pope has repudiated the National Socialist New European Order...
His speech is one long attack on everything we stand for.*--Classified
Gestapo report on Pius XII's 1942 Christmas Address

In the summer of 1941 the Nazi government introduced a sinister
new policy to deal with resistance to their rule in occupied France.
Upon capture, Frenchmen simply disappeared. No court, no
appeal, no power or person could account for their whereabouts. The
policy was called *Nacht und Nebel*, Night and Fog, because it could
happen to anyone, at any time, for no reason. This odious policy cast
dread over occupied populations and silenced many with an ominous
terror of the unknown. Overt resistance diminished.

The "Night and Fog" policy's success was later applied to Nazism's
greatest goal, the destruction of European Jewry. No outside authority
would learn of the plan and no appeal would be heard. So classified
was this policy that no written document about its origin has ever
been found. Such was the atmosphere in Nazi-occupied Europe. How,
in this suspicious, deceptive, and capriciously lawless atmosphere did
the Vatican, that is, the Pope and his hierarchy, function? How could
the Vatican intervene on behalf of the persecuted Jews in such an
atmosphere, a predicament the Vatican had battled since the onset of
Nazi power?

Vatican actions to help the Jews under Nazi rule from 1933 to 1945 were
at once diplomatic and formal, but also adroitly subtle and covert. In
the end, the Vatican was the most successful government entity to act
on behalf of Jews during the entire period.

To understand this nuanced policy, we'll first need to review the Vatican's relationship with pre-war Nazi Germany. The Vatican relentlessly emphasized racial equality while actively assisting Jewish emigration from increasing persecution. Secondly, we'll examine the Vatican's wartime responses to the persecution and murder of Jews in various Axis countries, where dictatorial rule was by no means uniform. Once the Vatican realized that Jewish lives were at stake, that every method of intervention was a matter of life or death, it spared no effort to rescue them. As the Papal Nuncio to Turkey (who saved 20,000 Jews in the Balkans), Cardinal Angelo Roncalli, later John XXIII, stated, "I simply carried out the Pope's orders, first and foremost to save human lives." By analyzing historical realities we can establish how effective these policies were.

The Vatican represented a Church that taught the common dignity and equality of man. This belief governed all its policy statements, initiatives, and actions. This fundamental belief was the core conflict between the Vatican and the Nazi Reich. Repeated Vatican proclamations about the universal family of man flew in the face of Hitler's "scientific anti-Semitism". Every Papal statement against Hitler's racial Darwinism, no matter how refined or oblique, was immediately understood by the adversary, as the Nazi Secretary of State Ernst von Weizsäacker confirmed, "To be sure, the Vatican expresses itself in general terms, but it is perfectly clear who is meant."

One belief, universal and equal, could not coexist with the other, racial and supremacist. It paid for its limited freedom of action by constant Nazi harassment, arrests, and executions of its priests and churchmen. An SS document, *Rassenpolitik*, maintained, "A philosophy that assumes human equality... is an error or a conscious lie." The Vatican continued not only to prime its ideas at every turn, but also thereby laid the groundwork for all its subsequent actions on behalf of the Jews.

Upon their accession to power, the Nazis simply and clearly defined their program. They would avenge the humiliations of the Versailles treaty, erase the corrupt Weimar democracy, and end the horrendous joblessness and hunger of depression. Hitler would give the German his pride back.

The Nazis spoke of reclaiming a wondrous, distant and mystic Aryan past. In this golden, pre-Christian age the simple Volksgemeinschaft, or racial community, honest and forthright, characterized what it meant to be born of pure German blood. Brave men protected fair-haired women who cared for home and children. What destroyed this era of virtue? Treason. Betrayal. The parasitic mongrel race, the decadent and rootless Jew, stabbed the German army in the back in the World War. Such perfidious betrayal heralded the advent of race-defiling, post-war cosmopolitanism as embodied in "the Church, Liberalism, Bolshevism, and Jewry," according once again to Rassenpolitik. But for National Socialism, with its roots in German blood and heritage, the German Volk would have succumbed. God himself "sent" Adolf Hitler to save Germany. Hitler alone knew how to deal with the Jew. Opposed to this siren song, which tempted millions of impoverished, shamed, and despairing Germans, the Vatican knew it had to take care, or it would lose any influence it had.

Hitler firmly believed that British propaganda had undermined the German war effort in World War I. He observed the Allies explain their cause in easily understood mottos: defeat the Hun and world liberty. He recalled the Germans had none. Together with his propaganda minister Dr. Joseph Goebbels he spread his racial superiority concepts. They employed what by all accounts was incredibly advanced usage of new communications technologies in radio, film, theater and literature. With insights from the new science of psychology, the Nazis manipulated the German mentality. For example, Leni Riefenstahl's film "Triumph of the Will" recorded Hitler's triumphant arrival at the first Nazi party congress as if he were a victorious Roman Emperor. Hitler, filmed amid resounding music, Klieg lights and cheering soldiers shouting "SiegHeil" (Hail Victory), embodied victories to come. A banner in every Nazi rally hall proclaimed, "*Die Juden sind unser Unglück* "(The Jews are our Misfortune). One leader with one goal demanded total submission. No other belief system could co-exist with this exclusionary racism.

Cardinal Eugenio Pacelli, later Pius XII, identified this threat. Cardinal Pacelli was the papal nuncio (ambassador) to the German Kingdom of Bavaria from 1917 through the Weimar years. He saw at first hand the sufferings of the German people. He saw as well that Nazi victory would kill the patient. Philosophically, he was committed to the dignity of each person, and that "the Church will never come to terms with Nazis as long as they persist in their racial philosophy". Together with Pope Pius XI, he carefully assessed the growing Nazi power.

Pacelli became Papal Secretary of State in 1929 and Vatican City was recognized by Italy as an independent state under the Lateran Treaty. The Vatican codified its new international relationships at this time with numerous national concordats (treaties). These concordats established the ground rules whereby the Vatican functioned in a given country. Vatican diplomacy was conducted via a hierarchy of papal nuncios (ambassadors) and apostolic delegates (consuls) who worked through local bishops. Papal guidance was communicated via encyclicals, a Latin text on a given theme. These were reprinted in the vernacular and read out from pulpits in a given country. Also, Radio Vatican was created in 1931, primarily in response to Italian fascist efforts to undermine papal rights guaranteed under the Lateran Treaty.

The Vatican reached a concordat with Germany in 1933. Within months the Nazis began to violate its principles. Whereas against the Jews the Nazis were harsh and overt, against the Church they concocted outrageous allegations of sexual deviancy and financial irregularities among Catholic clergy and closed Catholic schools, institutes, and newspapers. The Nazis thus sought to undermine Catholic teaching authority and insidiously diminish Catholic ability to counter Nazi claims on anyone's behalf. In response, Cardinal Pacelli authored and Pius XI proclaimed the only encyclical ever written in the German language, *Mit Brennender Sorge* (With Burning Anguish). It denounced Nazi duplicity and attempts to undermine agreed rules and usurp Catholic education. The Catholic position of the equality of mankind was restated. As Pacelli clearly stated in 1935 to 250,000 pilgrims at Lourdes, France, "They are in reality only miserable plagiarists who dress up old errors with new tinsel. It does not make any difference whether they flock to banners of social revolution or.... whether they are possessed by the superstition of race and blood cult," so again in the encyclical "... the enemies of the Church, who think their time has come, will see that their joy was premature, and they may close the grave they dug," and again, "whoever follows that so-called pre-Christian Germanic conception of a dark and impersonal destiny for the personal God... denies the Wisdom and Providence of God... Neither is he a believer in God."

Even more powerfully, *Mit Brennender Sorge* proclaimed against the "aggressive paganism" that "should any man dare in sacrilegious disregard for the essential difference between God and his creature... to place a mortal, were he the greatest of all times, by the side of, or over, or against, Christ, he would be called a prophet of nothingness."

The Nazis understood immediately who was meant by this text. *Mit Brennender Sorge* undercut racial superiority, indeed it denounced the German Savior, Adolf Hitler, and so the Nazi claim to rule. The Nazis moved rapidly to block its distribution, confiscating copies, arresting and sending to concentration camps printers who produced the document and priests who read it. In Dresden copies of the encyclical were passed hand to hand. The conflict lines were drawn for greater battles to come. Pius XI summarized in his 1937 Christmas address, "To call things by their real name: in Germany it is religious persecution... it is a persecution lacking neither force nor violence, neither oppression nor threats, neither sly craftiness nor lying."

Every Catholic defense of the defenseless in Germany was met with immediate retaliation. For example, a 1934 Nazi film documentary, *Das ein ohne Leben*, introduced a euthanasia program. Using apparent scientific rationality, the film proposed to eliminate "beings without life", the mentally handicapped, and devote money thus saved to national revitalization. Catholics resoundingly pilloried this hideous first step in 'race purification'. When Bishop Clemens Graf von Galen of Münster denounced the program, his diocesan priests were rounded up and sent to concentration camps, where many would die. As with the disabled, so with the Jews, persecution grew. Pacelli implored bishops of the world to encourage their governments to admit the half-million Jews seeking to flee Nazi Germany, but even America declined significant help. The Vatican encouraged the development of national relief foundations for Jews, of food shipments, of financial assistance, of material help, and again and again insisted that equal rights be respected. Pacelli knew that mere words would not stop the Nazis, action was required.

Upon his succession to the Papacy in 1939, among Pius XII's first acts was to raise an Asian, two Africans, and an Indian to the bishopric. The point was not lost on the Nazis, who closed churches, schools, and arrested priests. His first encyclical *Summi Pontificus* again condemned racism, reminding that "there is neither Gentile nor Jew". It too was confiscated. While Hitler could proclaim his views to millions via the ingenious *Volksempfänger*, the 'people's radio' he had mass-produced, the Germans were forbidden on pain of imprisonment, and later death, to listen to Radio Vatican.

Vatican policy in the pre-war years was to assist German Jewish 'emigration'; to help Jews escape the tightening Nazi noose. The Nazis stripped away Jewish rights through the Nuremberg Laws. Jews were persecuted and expropriated, yet no country would take them in large numbers as refugees, despite Vatican pleas and admonitions for help. Pius proposed to all ambassadors to the Vatican that their countries admit Jewish refugees. Small numbers were accepted throughout the world. Pius even appealed to Palestine's British authorities. He proposed a peace conference to avoid war, but no major power agreed to come. He personally worked to have thousands of Jews admitted to Brazil. Then he appealed to all bishops to encourage their governments to help. Vatican emissaries throughout the world worked wherever they had influence to encourage nations to accept refugees. As with all the dozens of protests he formally filed as nuncio, he continued to denounce Nazi Jewish policy. The nuncio in Berlin, Archbishop Cesare Orsenigo, repeatedly intervened in Jewish cases. The Pope continually re-emphasized the theme of the equality of man, while he actively worked personally and through his nuncios and bishops on behalf of the persecuted. Alone amidst governments who would not see or help, he struggled to find escape hatches for the persecuted, vilified scapegoats of Europe.

When the war broke out, Nazi themes changed. Now they claimed to be the last bulwark of civilization against Bolshevism. The Nazis saw the Jew behind the Red menace.

The Vatican declared its neutrality. As neutrals the Vatican could continue to function with formal representatives in warring countries. It could, as in the First World War, ensure that prisoners were identified and families notified. Indeed, it rescued several thousand Jews who were stranded at sea and transferred them to encampments in southern Italy, where they survived the war. It could assure the movement of emergency food and communication between families, prisoners, and their native countries. It could file diplomatic protests against excesses where they could be identified, and privately argue individual cases. Above all, it could try to mediate among enemies, and communicate diplomatic and other initiatives for those who could not. Indeed, the Vatican facilitated one German anti-Nazi scheme which foundered when the British refused to communicate, even through Vatican intermediaries. As Vatican peace initiatives failed, the fate of the Jews became even more tenuous.

Jews were corralled into ghettos, where they died through neglect and malnutrition. They were soon deported to unknown destinations. Where even in wartime private Vatican entreaties sometimes worked to free concentration camp inmates, in the case of the Jews, however, no formal efforts succeeded. By late 1941 Jews were rumored to have been liquidated behind Eastern combat zones. Indeed, the nuncio to Berlin commented with increasing perplexity that in any Jewish case he was now simply ignored by Nazi authorities. Vatican's efforts to assist European Jewry under direct Nazi control became increasingly difficult, and no one could pinpoint what had brought about this change. Casimir Papee, Polish ambassador to the Vatican, referring to the liquidation of the Warsaw Ghetto, commented that when even old Jewish men, women, and children were being beaten and brutally deported to the East, grave doubts about their ultimate destination could be inferred.

The Vatican's wartime policy sought to prevent Jewish deportation to "the East". What was the ultimate destination of the Jews? Repeated formal complaints in Berlin merited nothing, neither by the Vatican, the Red Cross, nor any neutral entity. No power could to halt these obsessive, ominous deportations, about which no appeal would be heard.

Pius intuited from the hideous treatment of the Jews in the ghettos and the transport stations that lives were at stake. He sent a secret letter, *Opere Et Caritate* (by Work and Love) to the Catholic bishops of Europe. It commanded them to help those who 'suffered racial discrimination at the hands of the Nazis', in any way that would save them.

The truth behind the mysterious deportations is now known. Reinhard Heydrich, the SS Reich Protector in conquered Czechoslovakia, introduced Hitler's final solution at the Wannsee conference of January 1942. The Nazi leadership agreed to secretly deport and then murder Europe's Jews in remote camps located in occupied Eastern Europe. The earlier *Nacht und Nebel* plan had been effective. So too the Final Solution would work by Night and Fog, and no appeal would be heard. This is why the Vatican's appeals for the Jews fell on deaf ears.

In a quixotic Allied attempt to incite resistance, Heydrich, the "Butcher of Prague", was ambushed there in 1942 by Czech parachutists. Hitler ordered a horrific slaughter, massacring or deporting some 9,000 people to avenge him. Lidice, a Czech village, was plowed, Carthage-like, from the face of the earth. When in 1942 Dutch bishops "in consort with Holy Father" denounced Nazism's "barbarous deportation of the Jews", Hitler responded by rounding up even those Jews who converted to Catholicism. Pius XII was stunned. He observed that had he himself made the proclamation, 200,000 would have been taken, rather than 40,000. The Nazis added, "No intervention will be considered." They communicated a brutal and cynical message. Pius, to succeed in saving lives, had to act with greater discretion. Indeed, in light of the terrible retaliations in the Netherlands and Poland before it, Jewish organizations and European bishops implored the Vatican to be more circumspect. Pius, though he wanted to "speak words of fire," knew that such "would make the fate of the wretches even worse." In a mid-war letter to Cardinal Konrad von Preysing, Bishop of Berlin, Pius said, "We give to the pastors who are working on the local level the duty of determining if and to what degree the danger of reprisals occasioned by episcopal declarations...seems to advise caution, to avoid greater evil, despite alleged reasons urging the contrary."

Pius XII saw how fruitless symbolic or quixotic actions were, not to mention formal or public protests. As in the case of the Dutch bishops, public actions were paid for in vats of blood through Nazi revenge. Thus, to save the Jews, he acted covertly. Pius gave secret orders to his nuncios to hide Jews in monasteries, to issue false baptismal certificates, to affect escapes, and to influence governments. They were to pay money, give medicine and food where possible, establish homes, camps, false identities, even false functions for their suffering Jewish brethren. (300 Papal Guards were disguised Jews!) Pius even spent his personal inheritance to save Jews being blackmailed by the Gestapo, not to mention hiding 3000 Jews in his private residence at Castel Gandolfo.

Across Europe, in every country where German deportation orders were issued, the Vatican fought, by fair means and foul, through the nuncios, the bishops, and through their proclamations to the faithful. They prevailed far more in Axis client states than where Nazis ruled directly. Cardinal Roncalli, the papal nuncio to Turkey, who saved some twenty thousand Jews marked for death in the Balkans, declared all he did was "known to the Holy See." Playing for time in Hungary, the Pope interceded with Admiral Horthy, whose government swayed to and fro with German demands for compliance; even delivering 2000 Vatican safe-conduct passes to Jews en route to Mauthausen. Vichy was appealed to. Archbishop Jules-Géraud Saliège of Toulouse denounced the deportations and reminded his flock that "the Jews are our brothers. They belong to mankind. No Christian can forget that!" In Spain, thousands of Jews were allowed to cross over the border from France, thus saving them. Italian soldiers were influenced to allow Jews to escape deportation orders, so much so that the order was considered useless. Cardinal Luigi Maglione "expressed the Holy See's thinking" on the deportations to the Slovakian government, and "vigorously protested the treatment recently inflicted on hundreds of Jewish women..." Regrettably, Vatican appeals to Allied countries to admit Jews often fell on deaf ears.

On and on the Vatican appealed, pled, cajoled, implored and acted, openly and secretly where necessary. Sometimes successful, often not, it was not for want of trying. Even up to February 1945, in Berlin, Archbishop Orsenigo sought to alleviate Jewish suffering. The nuncio in Bratislava was told to remain in place, in the ruins, so long as "some charity could be done."

Throughout the period of National Socialist rule, the Vatican intervened in any and every way that which offered possible success in saving Jewish lives. In pre-war Germany, the Vatican fought on behalf of Jewish refugees. Formal concordats allowed the hierarchy to function, to influence, and to act to relieve the sufferings of Jews.

With the war, the Vatican remained neutral. This allowed it to function in occupied Europe, while nevertheless covertly helping the Jews, saving lives where possible. Without the treaties, Pius could not continue to communicate with his representatives who understood the local conditions better, which allowed for fine- tuning a policy which had to be correct, since lives were at stake. Nuncios and bishops "on station" were in a better position to help in realistic ways, and could remain on duty as representatives of a neutral government. Their actions, directed by Pius XII, were consistent; reminding the faithful that racism "was incompatible with the teachings of the Catholic Church." The hierarchy took any action it could to save Jews, be it hiding, forging documents, funding, assisting, or physically taking the defenseless away to safety. The Catholic principle of the common dignity of man provoked action, while Pius steered it.

Poignantly, Chief Rabbi Isaac Herzog of Palestine wrote in February 1945, "The people of Israel will never forget what His Holiness and his illustrious delegates… are doing for our unfortunate brothers and sisters." Three months after the war's end, a petition of some 20,000 Jewish survivors reached the Vatican. "Allow us to ask the great honor of being able to thank personally His Holiness for the generosity he has shown us when we were persecuted during the terrible period of Nazi Fascism." Indeed Pinchas Lapide, Israeli Consul to the Vatican, summarized, "We Jews are a grateful people. No Pope in history has ever been thanked more heartily by Jews for having saved or helped their brethren in distress."

In the end, it is estimated that some 860,000 Jewish lives were saved by the actions of the Catholic Church. Of course, there is no standard whereby to judge of the sufficiency of so many saved while so many died. Who, looking back, could not have hoped for more rescues? Certainly the Pope did, who watched his many efforts wax and wane. Yet in light of all that was done, perhaps the Jewish proverb that he who saves a single life, saves the world, should suffice.

Inspired by a young American soldier who shot the lock off a transit concentration camp in southern Germany in 1945. He was in my father-in-law's company.

SET THE PRISONERS FREE

B y chance we met one autumn day, now many years ago.
    My life was in a hurry, while his seemed sage and slow.

The old man was a soldier once, who fought beyond the sea.
Said he, "I saw some sad, sad things that no boy ought to see.

We were at war with Germany, and we were tough and lean.
I'd lied so I could join the fight, for I was seventeen.

We jumped from planes at Normandy, and we were brash and clever.
    We thought the war would end quite soon, and we would live forever.

But war is not what you expect, not wholesome, pure and clean.
For I shot the lock once, off a gate, when I was seventeen.

It was a lock not for a camp of captured men from battle,
But a stall for children, women, men packed in like cattle.

Eyes so sunken they seemed dead; bodies ghostly white;
Naked murdered innocents who once were whole and bright.

I gave a guy a candy bar, so sick he was and thin.
He smiled for joy, his last on earth; my love had done him in.

I can't tell you anymore, yet I see it every day.
What happened at that transit camp will never go away."

I waited for an ending, I waited for the rest.

He said not one more single word, but what he had confessed.

Those murdered there so long ago, still lived on in his eyes.
Which even now with years gone by could make another cry.

Do you wonder where they are now, those killed in fog and gloom?
Are they here among us, but silent in this room?

Are they haunted guests who whisper that we not forget?
There's one at least who hears them still, whose eyes with mine
once met.

The old man went beyond the sea, a boy who sought the war,
And came back a young soldier with a mental battle scar.

Yes, we should all remember, and we should not forget
How evil lives among us, and evil's with us yet.

For the sake of all our children, what that soldier's eyes have seen,
Should never, ever, have a chance to happen yet again.

A glisten of remembrance, a sorrow felt and keen,
Should never happen to a boy who's only seventeen.

Father Dondi

Whoever first called him Father Dondi must have met him in the 1950's. That's when the comic strip by that name appeared. Dondi, in the comic strip, was a lost little Italian orphan boy who was adopted by the US Army as it fought up the Italian peninsula. He was kind, gentle, friendly to all, and like his guardians loved America. What we knew was that Father Dondi loved America. We never heard anything he said, either officially, or when we met him on the American military post in Italy, which didn't end with an ode to what a great place America was and that American people were wonderful beyond measure.

One day, he was talking to us after church. Our boys asked him what the red buttons on his cassock meant. He told us a story that went well beyond his red buttons, for he told us of how he was once good and brave like Dondi, only in real life.

He studied theology as a seminarian in Rome during the war. If you graduate from a Roman academy, you can wear red buttons on your cassock. One day the rector of the school came to him and said he needed all of their second cassocks. Intrigued, since with wartime shortages they had only two cassocks, they asked the reason. "The Holy Father says we are going to get new seminarians, and they have no cassocks."

When the new seminarians arrived, they not only had no cassocks, but no idea of Catholicism. "These fellows are Jews, and are on the run from the Nazi Fascists."

Fear can sometimes freeze any action, for good or wrong. Father was quite honest. He admitted that every day when he remembered the Jews were there, in hiding outside of the Vatican, he knew fear. If he and his classmates were betrayed, simple knowledge of an escapee meant a concentration camp or death. Yet moreover he was intensely sad about the stark horrors the Jewish refugees themselves must have been going through. Then one day, which dawned like any other in occupied Rome, the rector came in, with associates carrying their extra cassocks. He feared the worst.

"You may have these back, gentlemen. Their former owners are now in Palestine. They want to convey their thanks for your hospitality!"

A Valentine Story

How murder became state policy, but how a little girl survived.

L ove, as the legend of St. Valentine reminds us, triumphs where evil is worst. Ancient Rome's Valentine story is eternal. It tells of a priest who secretly married Roman lovers when marriage was outlawed by a mad Emperor in order to force men into his army. It is eternal because fables carry eternal truths through time.

It was Adolf Hitler who in September 1939 ordered the adoption of an involuntary euthanasia program aimed at killing all those who were considered "unworthy of life," an expression that originated with the title of a book published in 1920 by Karl Binding, a retired professor of law, and Alfred Hoche, a psychiatrist at the University of Freiburg. The compulsory sterilization of individuals with serious mental and physical conditions, the severely disabled, the mentally ill, and the incurably sick, was already widespread in many countries. The Nazis extended these eugenic practices to mass murder. They concluded that without quality of life, these lesser beings should not take away resources from the physically healthy, the fit, and the racially pure. After all, they argued, better a school for the young, bright and happy, than an institute for the insane. Who could argue with that?

The plan to secretly murder those undesirables, those *dasein ohne Leben,* beings without life, was euphemistically named the *Charitable Foundation for Cure and Institutional Care.* This program was later labeled Aktion T4 or the T-4 program, after the villa at Tiergartenstrasse 4, in Berlin, from which it was directed. Although the T-4 Program was carried out in the darkest secrecy, slowly its existence came to be whispered about. It took one bishop, Clemens August Graf von Galen of Münster, Germany, to loudly, specifically, and heroically denounce the program from his pulpit. It was, he declared, contrary to Christian principles of the Gospel of Life. In those early days, even Hitler backed down against such a tidal wave of opposition. The T-4 program went underground, to be reborn during the Second World War.

In 1943, our friend Renate's sister Melanie was born in a small German country town with what today we call Down's Syndrome. Her mother was terrified, for if her baby came to the attention of Nazi zealots, Melanie would be taken away and gassed. So it was that Renate, herself just a few years older than her baby sister, was told to play with her only at home, and never to talk about her in town. After two more years, the Nazi terror came to an end. Melanie could play wherever she wanted. She was loved, and is loved, to this day. She makes people happy by her eternal joy of life.

Renate met and fell in love with Georg at the ancient, tree-lined campus of Martin Luther University in Halle, Germany. He was studying to become a doctor. As the fortunes of post-war politics hardened, the border between Renate's West and Georg's East turned into an impassible Iron Curtain. Yet Renate loved Georg, and chose to return to him in the East. To do so meant to enter the police state of Communist East Germany, in which a government of surveillance, arbitrary arrest, anti-religion, and class warfare ruled. She was treated worse than a criminal by the Communists. She was first considered a spy, and tormented by every act of the master state that the new red Nazis could muster. Yet return she did, for she loved the man who became her husband. Georg was never happier, for he married Renate and they are, to this day, happily married.

Of course the Wall finally came down. Now the doctor and Renate can visit with the families of his successful and happy children, for they are free to travel and do what they like. Moreover, this is why the Valentine story will always remain with us. Love protected Melanie until the Nazi lies were only a memory. Love prevailed even when to marry meant to risk life under a police state. In this case, that better tomorrow finally came, too. And after all, isn't that how love stories end?

ITALIAN INCIDENT

While traveling the back roads of Italy, we'd stop here and there to strike up a conversation with local people. I wanted to practice my brand-new Italian, and maybe learn something. If anything, my energy-bursting three sons needed a break now and then. We drove to a town at the foothills of the magnificent Dolomite mountains. My boys ran off to go see where the rushing water noises were coming from.

Only a block from where we parked, they came upon an utterly captivating mountain stream cascading down from its source high above. As we neared the river, we saw a walkway that followed the road paralleling the stream. The walkway was breath taking, with flowering trees planted at some 20-foot intervals the entire length of the road, as far as the eye could see. Then I noted something on each tree. A small photograph of a different person was attached at eye level. Around the photograph was a hand-made noose, like they use in executions. Each person's photo carried the message, "Killed by Nazi soldiers." I was stunned.

Not wanting to scare the boys, who wouldn't understand, I looked for someone to explain what had happened. A passing Italian lady told us this story.

"The war was almost over. The Nazis were retreating up into the mountains to go home to Germany. They would kill anybody they even thought resisted them. In fact, most of these people memorialized on these trees were murdered when a partisan group ambushed the Germans north of here in the mountains. The German officer announced to the town that if a German is killed in front of a house, everyone in the whole building will be killed in revenge."

This incredible tale came too quickly, too powerfully to comprehend. Then she continued, "I can tell you our story. We don't live on a main street. My mother, me and my sister were home one night when we heard a shot. Normally we little kids went to bed early. Suddenly Mamma burst into the room, and got my sister and me up. 'Get water! Get buckets of water!' Mamma screamed. 'Somebody shot a German in the street near our front door. We've got to get him out of there.' So we ran madly outside, and Mamma and my sister hauled his body into a ditch in the wood way behind our house. I slapped the sidewalk with the mop, cleaning up the blood for what seemed to be hours. When I was finished, Mamma in a hushed voice screamed at me to get inside, 'Tell no one, ever!'"

THE PAINTER'S TALE

❝ Would you be so kind as to use your German language skills to find this place?" asked our friend, herself of Italian birth, now American, showing us a photocopy of her father's World War II prisoner identification card. He had been held in a German POW camp for the last two years of that war. Now, in the 1980s, his story became a part of my family's adventures.

After calls to several police colleagues, we accomplished the quest, and there the matter rested until I was called again.

"Could you please take my father back to this place?"

Who could say no? So, on a brisk Saturday, my family and I, together with our friend and her father, set off through a rarely-visited industrial region near the town of Merzig in Germany.

Carlo, Adriana's father, was a painter drafted into the army whose unit was part of the Italian occupation army in Albania. Remote, impoverished Albania was one of the few Mussolini-conquered lands of Europe. They were so far from their headquarters they hadn't heard that their country had switched sides. Thus, when the German *Wehrmacht* arrived, they were all taken prisoner, and shipped off to a cold, distant mine in north-central Germany. He and his comrades became slave laborers for the Third Reich.

Upon our arrival at this location, high up on a hill overlooking a small village below, we saw that the wooden barracks he remembered had disappeared. Replacing them were concrete barracks, of the same shape, bearing the same atmosphere of sorrow and suppressed pain. Here, in the modern Germany of the 1980's, the mentally deficient were housed. They seemed to simply dwell in these green block barracks, staring out from their concrete doorsteps into a melancholy existence.

I didn't need to ask anyone where the entrance to the mine had been. A giant concrete slab covered the pit entrance that once held a huge tower which ferried loads of slaves up and down into the blackness below.

Carlo, upon seeing the slab, asked to be alone. He walked off a distance by himself, to be away from the curious, bizarre, and sad people surrounding our tiny expedition. He stayed away for some time. When at last we found him again, to continue on our way, he told us his story.

"When I saw this slab of concrete over there, I remembered my time here." His face was streaked with tears, and he seemed unable to continue at first, but then said, "We lived in wooden barracks, raised off the ground by foot-tall wooden stilts. Every day we'd have a formation, then be taken to these mines to work for hours. Our only break to this routine was when they marched us under guard down the hill into town, to a church on Sunday. We didn't understand the priest, but we understood the Mass."

Adriana told us later she'd never heard his story before.

He continued, "One day, we woke up not to a bugle but to general chaos. The guards were gone! We stumbled around like blind men, didn't know what to do. Then someone said, 'Let's go ask Father in town what to do, he'll know.' As a mob we walked down the hill again. At the base of the hill, we blundered into SS soldiers, who by chance had stopped there that morning in retreat from the oncoming Americans. The SS men opened fire on us with machine pistols, and we all ran back up the hill, like madmen possessed. They chased us, shooting and killing! It was terrifying, and many men dived under the barracks to hide. Then the SS men threw hand grenades under the buildings, blowing up those who were hiding, burning some barracks, and slaughtering everyone. I saw this myself from the forest, which used to be there. I'd run past the barracks with some friends, and once we thought we were safe in the woods we turned back to see what had happened. Then we just ran for our lives, and hid for days, starving in the woods until we surrendered again to the Americans."

By now, my wife and Adriana were in tears, our boys didn't know what to think of the strange place where people seemed to dwell, not live, and this old man with us who was so very sad.

Carlo was intensely thankful he could see this place again. He gave us a gift the next year. It was a landscape painting of a peaceful, pastoral view. I'd never asked what kind of painter he was.

Dead Men's Bells

The German grandfather offered to take me and my three boys out on a '*Spaziergang*' (a walk) in the forest. A walk on a brisk, but occasionally rainy day through gloomy, bird-filled forests seemed almost the epitome of what it meant to be Germanic. Off we went, with the boys, my oldest at eight, running dead ahead. As we quietly entered the husky, hard-wood trees, unusual for that part of West Germany, he asked, "Was your father ever in World War II?"

I said yes, in the Navy against Japan.

"I was in Russia." We walked a while further, and then he added, "I was a vehicle mechanic with a *Waffen SS* unit."

These were the armed combat units devised by the Nazis to finally become the new German Army, since Hitler utterly distrusted the traditional *Wehrmacht*.

"Russia was terrible. You could freeze even your eyelids off. Men died from any wound not treated, because of gangrene. And the frostbite! *Fürchterlich!* Even vehicle oil froze, and weapon oil. We had no coats for winter."

As soon as we came into a clearing, he called the boys back. Our oldest spoke German, and led his brothers in a line back to us through the grasses. "Boys, do you see this plant?"

We Americans knew it as foxglove, but I translated its German word, *Fingerhut*.

"*Fingerhut?*" laughed my oldest, "Finger hat? Why would I put them on my finger?"

The old man continued, "These are deadly in every way. It is important to tell children so they aren't deceived and think you can play with them."

I did a translation, and the boys naturally reacted as if they'd found a snake growing on a vine. "We'll watch out Daddy!" they cried, and ran back ahead.

"Do you know I never knew about the murder of the Jews during the war?" he began as soon as we were alone and it was quiet again. "I remember when I found out, but I didn't believe it."

His story had taken a new twist, for I said quite literally nothing.

"It was Christmas, 1943, and I was on the military leave train going home. We pulled into Warsaw. When the doors opened to let in troops, a wild gust of winter wind and snow rushed through every corner of the cabins. Through the whiteness emerged a couple of men trying to get into our cabin which until then was warm.

"'Close the door behind you,' I called as they entered, and only then noticed that one of them was my former comrade from SS Basic Military School. He answered in a confusion of words and I knew right away he was absolutely drunk. He had joined the '*Totenkopf*' (Death's Head) unit, and was stationed somewhere in conquered Poland. I hadn't seen him since our training days, and wondered what had happened to him and others who had chosen that sort of military police unit.

"'So what are you up to these days?' I asked him as he found his seat and threw his bags overhead.

"'We're killing them all!' he screamed, 'every last one of the Jews and Communists we get! We're killing them all!'

"I thought he was making up brave stories because he knew we were the ones really fighting the Red Army and winter, while he spent the war in this rear area chasing refugees and deserters. All of us who were coming from the front laughed or scorned his drunken monologue.

"'No!' He insisted. 'No, we are killing every one we get our hands on. You don't even know!' And with that, he curled up and fell asleep, and we left him alone.

"'Damned drunk' in our opinion, who never fought real soldiers. And to lie about shooting as if he were in a war, too. Good, let him sleep. Liar. Only later we found out they really were killing them all."

We said nothing more until we got home, and that was the end.

Only years later I discovered that foxglove is also called Dead Men's Bells. You need to warn children, because what appears harmless can have terrible consequences.

A Thought About Modern War

We are in war, but we aren't at war.-- UN Observer, Bosnia, 1999

In the Field Hospital

Only once in his life did Dan ever win anything. He won the lottery. He won the national military draft lottery, and his prize was a trip to the Vietnam War as a combat infantryman. Having grown up in the New York City metropolitan area, the jungles of Vietnam were the most distant, different, least known and horrifying places an Italian-American from the huge urban sprawl could possibly go. Yet go he did, at the height of the tense and fearful period of the Tet Offensive.

Dan's unit of the 101st Airborne Division was to deploy near the city of Hue. Gathering one crisp dawn before the sweltering, unforgiving, relentless heat of Vietnam descended, they took off in Huey helicopters carrying some six men each. Covering the many miles in a ride which smelled of gasoline, they approached the LZ, or landing zone clearing. There they'd rapidly descend, exit the 'chopper, and disappear into the jungle for a patrol.

Upon landing, the men bounded out as best they could with their immense rucksacks on their backs. They ran a couple yards, then fell to the ground. When the helicopters departed, the world exploded with gunfire from the surrounding jungle. Rapid-fire Kalashnikov rifles from a Vietnamese ambush punctured the ground and shot past the Americans. "Get up, get up" screamed someone as several soldiers performed the only 'tactic' available, a direct assault.

Dan grabbed his partner and pulled him toward the tree line. "C'mon!" Dan's adrenalin shouted, but the man did not come. A red hole marked his forehead. He'd been hit, and killed.

"This is why no one ever got to know the other guys' names," Dan said. "Everybody had a nickname. I was Dodger, and there were other guys whose real names I don't think I ever knew. It protected us in a way. If you didn't even know someone's name, you felt a little less pain when he was killed. After all, that's what war's about, pain."

Dan left after his year as a combat infantryman in Vietnam. He returned stateside to become a military nurse and an officer. Yet the pain of war never really left him. This is why, I imagine, to lessen that of others, he went back to Vietnam for another year of war as a nurse anesthetist in a field hospital. He received in that emergency tent the shot, broken-boned, stabbed, blown-up, mangled, sucking-chest wounded, burned, shocked and terrified young Americans and Vietnamese. Day after day, in all weather conditions and without many medical necessities, he dealt with trying to stop the pain of the hellish danse macabre which arrived in all its forms without cease. If this were a novel, the symbolism would be considered too extreme. Yet it happened.

Dan also became an ordained minister of his church in later years while still on active duty in the military. He wanted to help others find God in the pains of this world. I've found it of profound significance that Pope Francis, leader of Dan's Church, declared the Church a sort of 'spiritual field hospital'. What a remarkable choice of expression. Dan is one of his medical officers.

COUNTERINTELLIGENCE: SEEING THROUGH THE ENEMY'S EYES

On a 50-mile front near Sedan, France, massed German armor circumvented the northern end of the Maginot Line in May 1940. Panic struck the French forces, which fled headlong from the Blitzkrieg. British Prime Minister Winston Churchill, visiting French leaders in Paris, asked the French commander-in-chief, "Where is the strategic reserve?"

"There is none," the commander replied.

Churchill said later, "I was dumb-founded. I admit this was one of the greatest surprises I have had in my life. Why had the British Government and the War Office not known about this?" This battlefield surprise rolled up the French Army and British Expeditionary Force, and pushed them to Dunkirk, France, and the sea.

Surprise on the battlefield is the event that men and women in combat fear most because surprise means dead soldiers. It was to preclude such surprise and assure victory that the principles of war evolved. Each principle of the U.S. Army - objective, offensive, mass, economy of force, maneuver, unity of command, security, simplicity, and surprise - helps to minimize the fog of war and assure victory.

The absence of a French reserve led to the fall of France. The Germans knew about this, but the British did not. What happened?

Such a question introduces the role of counterintelligence (CI) on the modern battlefield. CI analysts have in their arsenal two weapons of which they may not even be aware: the principles of war and operations security (OPSEC). The *Wuzi*, quoted by Sun Tzu, says, "What is called the right way is a return to fundamental principles; if conduct is not in accord with [the right way], although one's position is important and honorable, misfortune will overtake him."

The French and British spent years learning everything about the Germans. They knew to the last German soldier how many men the Germans could transport from Hanover to Aachen on a given day. The problem was that they never looked at themselves the way the Germans did. The Germans knew them even better than they knew themselves. The Germans knew that the French had violated the primary principle of war. An element of critical allied information was lost to the enemy collection threat. Good CI could have precluded this, and the battle in France could have ended differently.

What should have happened then? What could happen now?

CI must first evaluate U.S. operations. They must examine the United States though adversarial eyes and ask the questions about U.S. operations that an opponent would ask. CI must think like the adversary, looking at friendly operations from the outside inward.

Allied CI could have begun by asking, *What is critical to our operation?* What could compromise its success? Once they established the critical information parameters, they could compare it to Germany's ability to collect critical information. If there was no strategic reserve and if the Germans, once through the Maginot Line, could ravage communications and command centers, then the war was lost. CI could have identified this risk and helped to mitigate the German surprise.

 OPSEC was absent. They did not use the five-step process in which they can evaluate critical information against the collection threat to reveal vulnerabilities. Grave risk to the Allied side went unobserved. Allied CI should have analyzed the Allied position the same way the Germans did. They did not. They did not see themselves as if through the enemy's eyes. The Germans discovered a critical vulnerability and used the information for victory.

The study of this long-ago disaster has application today. Who evaluates the U.S. position on today's fields of conflict? Do we still underestimate the Somali tribesman's ability to collect intelligence against U.S. standard operating procedures? Do we still ignore military rules against the collection of laundry by locals in Bosnia, as we did in Vietnam? Are we so busy evaluating our enemies' orders of battle that we forget to look at our own and see ourselves as they see us?

CI has the principles of war. We know what it takes to assure victory and preclude surprise. We must look at our own operations in light of these principles because without a doubt our adversaries do. We must then apply the five-step Operations Security process. We must see where critical information is vulnerable to enemy collection capabilities and then make recommendations for countermeasures. As Winston Churchill ruefully observed, "What were we to think of the great French army? What was the Maginot Line for if not to economize troops, enabling large forces to be held in reserve for a counterstroke? But now there was no reserve."

The resulting disaster is now history. Can CI learn from this? To do so it must go back to the right way of the *Wuzi.* We must give our adversaries credit for being as smart as we are and see ourselves through their eyes. Never underestimate the enemy. Do it the right way.

Grenada Veteran's Promotion

Participants are authorized to wear the combat patch.

I met another veteran who didn't have a scar,
But who was a phony hero of a god-forsaken war.

He was told to take some memos to a staffer at the scene
Who was staying near the airport where the fighting all had been.

So he got there and he waited while two days came and went
Until he gave it up and went home 'cause his TDY was spent.

When he flew back to Miami his boss said there's a catch,
And directed that he sew on a Grenada Combat patch.

And so he did, that's what I saw,
But he never has forgot
The lie that caused the patch to be the symbol of the rot.

VICTORY IN PANAMA

Awards were granted for a firefight during the Panama Invasion.

As long as dead men do not count,
    Since corpses have no say,
    Anyone can be a victor when it comes to battle day.

A fight broke out or maybe not,
It doesn't really matter,
But the enemy was somehow there and later maybe scattered.

How many? I don't know, do you? Were you there? Who was?
But we've got a lot of victors and that is true, because
Because of what? Who cares? Do you? We won and hold the place.
Our "Pride of Arms" our "Victory" will in time all else erase.

Don't Let Terrorists Spread Fear

*So let me assert my firm belief that the only thing we have to fear is fear
itself - nameless, unreasoning, unjustified terror which paralyzes needed
efforts to convert retreat into advance.*--Franklin D. Roosevelt

Shortly after police alerted the nation that a vehicle license plate
was being sought in connection with the D.C. sniper, a citizen
reported it, and an arrest was made. The alleged killer was off the
street.

Recently, a waitress at a Shoney's Restaurant in Georgia notified
authorities of an apparent criminal discussion she overheard. Three
men seemed to be planning to bomb a building in Miami. After police
investigated, the bomb plot was alleged to be a hoax. In both cases,
these citizens did what any civic-minded American should do. They
reported a threat to the proper authorities. Such acts are our civic duty.

Not long ago my dad and I were comparing the surprise attack on
Pearl Harbor with the suicide assaults on the World Trade Center and
the Pentagon. "Something a lot of people don't remember about those
days," he reflected, "is that Americans were afraid. There were rumors
across the land that Japanese had landed in San Francisco, at Los
Angeles, and that saboteurs and spies were everywhere. Rumors spread
fear, and fear fanned more fear."

The greatest human emotion is fear, and the greatest fear is fear of
the unknown. It was for that very reason that President Roosevelt
reminded everyone that, "The only thing we have to fear is.... fear
itself."

You can't imagine what a calming effect the president's reassurance
had for everyone," dad said. "We were sucker punched at Pearl, but
pulled together for the fight to come. We believed the situation was
dangerous, but that the right people were doing their best to take care

of the nation. And it wouldn't be over till we finished it."

Today we too might believe the enemy appears to be everywhere. He seems capable of any number of horrific means of visiting destruction on us. We feel helpless to defend ourselves against an adversary we can neither see, nor identify, nor anticipate. We feel an unspecified dread. We don't feel safe anymore. That is just what the enemy wants us to feel.

My favorite quotation came the day after the September 11 attack. A German investigator, asked to comment on the apprehension of several al-Qaida terrorists in Hamburg, offered this matter-of-fact observation, "Don't forget. These people are criminals. Each of these terrorists has a face, a name, and an address."

That comment, echoing President Bush's determined assurance that we will patiently but relentlessly pursue these killers anywhere they may hide, did much to reassure Americans. But how, Americans ask, can we take part? We want to pull together, so what do we do?

The answer has been here all along; we've known it intuitively, but never until now really had an immediate need in this generation to act upon it. Working for the government, we know that loose lips sink ships. But now we know that our eyes catch spies... and the criminal killers they report to. Each of the terrorists has a face, a name, and an address, and now they too know fear. Their leaders have abandoned them, world law enforcement is seeking them, and every day more Americans become more astute in what to watch for and report. There are many practical hurdles to overcome, and the road won't be easy.

Whereas yesterday we weren't aware, today we know who to call if something just doesn't seem right. We help each other. Americans are pulling together. We watch our surroundings in ways we didn't before. We are protecting ourselves, informing ourselves, and not letting fear defeat us before we've entered the fight. No one today will turn away if a security problem seems to require a solution. We offer assistance to others and make sure someone takes action to protect us. If we see a better way, we speak up.

The only thing we have to fear is fear itself. Remember that every terrorist has a face, a name, and an address. We'll get them if we help each other. We are a quarter-billion Americans whose eyes are watching in restaurants, at gas stations, in the office, and on the road. Now the cowards who murdered our people really have something to fear. We are out to get them.

Christmas 2015, and Christmas 1915

Winter seems so far away, away beyond the sea.
I'm thinking now of Christmas days long past in
Germany.
Where Advent candles lit the weeks which heralded anew
The joyous day to follow when the *Christkind* comes in view.

Christmas is the time when Silent Night is best oft sung
To hosts who greet the Holy Night with peace and hope still young.
Christmas used to stop the wars, if only for a day
And brought a moment's respite to the guns and men who'd slay.

What is it that we hoped for when we celebrated then?
What is it that still draws a hope from conflict weary men?
We know we are far better than the calls to seek revenge,
Revenge that never worked before, why try it yet again?

We know that Christmas calls us to be better than the past
And seek the peace of Christmas, yea a peace that this time lasts.
That's what I hope this Christmas, that we no longer soldiers send--
Sons and daughters-- o'er the seas, like cut grass in the wind.

Christmas is a time when fathers, mothers should rejoice,
Because our better selves have come; and this time make the choice
To take a chance that dialogue will outdo even guns
To keep a family full next year, with no more missing sons.

We wish you all the very best that Christmas can yet bring
Of peace that no one takes away, about which prophets sing.
And here's a hope that never more will bullets our way fly,
Because we've fought hard to bring peace, at least we made the try.

*I was asked to give a presentation to a large military audience on how
to identify "Who's Out to Get You?" The purpose of the presentation
was to keep soldiers alert and alive in future deployments. I employed*

a deceptively light-hearted approach, the irony of which would better convey the deadly serious intent.

WHO'S OUT TO GET YOU?

"They're trying to kill me," Yossarian told him calmly.
"No one's trying to kill you," Clevinger cried.
"Then why are they shooting at me?" Yossarian asked.
"They're shooting at everyone," Clevinger answered. "They're trying to kill everyone."
"And what difference does that make?"--Joseph Heller, *Catch 22*

I first knew everyone was out to get me when they burned my ROTC building to the ground. All those other college kids looked like me, but they really were out to get me. So I joined the artillery when I was commissioned. A big shell can beat a Molotov any day. Then one day one of those giant 105 shells came whooshing my way and blew up a big tree, sending me flying. My own guys were trying to kill me! Not on purpose, of course, but still there I was, blown up anyway.

I thought deeply about this. Guys who didn't like me, and guys who did, were both trying to kill me. One group on purpose; one by mistake. It didn't make much difference though if I ended up dead. I wondered, was the entire world like this? I started to think so.

My presentation today is to show what happened in real combat; to show how even the basic trooper can learn from horrors others experienced, and stay alive. Specifically, Operations Security, OPSEC, is based on a "Healthy Paranoia". As internalized awareness, OPSEC allows the mission to succeed. No mission succeeds if we are dead.

As a young dad I read to my kids a lot from *Alice in Wonderland*. I went back to that book from time to time because it made so much sense. Here was Alice, who falls down the rabbit hole, and comes out in a place where nothing is as it seems. I thought, here is your standard trooper, fallen into Warfareland where nothing is as it seems. Think I am on to something here?

Alice went 'through the looking glass' to another world. She was mystified, lost, and wandering. A soldier on today's battlefield feels the same way. He's in a foreign land, can't speak the language, doesn't know who is on his side, and can't leave. He figures his main job is to stay alive, because he thinks everyone wants to kill him.

There is a way, then, for even the newest trooper to stay alive, even when everyone is out to get him, either through intent or default. That is OPSEC, or Operations Security. Remember, only live troopers can accomplish missions.

Everyone knows the five-step OPSEC process.1) Determine what's critical. 2) Know the threat. 3) Identify vulnerabilities. 4) Assess risk. 5) Create countermeasures. With a certain healthy paranoia, OPSEC will become as normal as breathing. Believe that, and you are halfway there. Exercise healthy paranoia, and you are there.

Sure, you're thinking, sure. But think about it a minute! All you have to do is believe that everyone is out to get you, and you will survive! Let me give you some tips and some stories that prove the points, then decide for yourself!

Step One: What is critical to protect?
Answer: Your life.

If you are dead, it doesn't matter much what steps two through five are, does it? Whether your cause is noble or not, being alive is very important to your mission. If everyone is out to get you, remember that and stay alive. Stay alert, stay alive. But what should the hapless trooper be alert to?
Step Two: The threat. Who is out to get you?
Answer: Everyone.

"Who are you?" asked the Caterpillar.

"I think, you ought to tell me who you are, first.'

'Why?' said the Caterpillar.

Here was another puzzling question; and as Alice could not think of any good reason, and as the Caterpillar seemed to be in a very unpleasant state of mind, she turned away.

There is the enemy who wants to kill you. There are also your friends, who can kill you through inattention and laziness. For example, if your friends repeat the same practices: the same patrol routes, the same landing zones, the same time for chow, the enemy can figure it out, and kill you. There is an old truism: don't let your raid turn into their ambush. That's why we call both friend and enemy together "the adversary." How can we learn about our adversary?

Here are some strange stories to consider.

A baker delivered a covered tray to some auto mechanics. They in turn delivered a car to a factory. They entered by means of a key given to them by a secret confederate inside. The tray, of course, was filled with explosives. The mechanics put the dynamite into a car which became a bomb. The factory was blasted sky high; the perpetrators escaped.

Or consider this. A weird, elderly man climbed towers to study architecture. From these towers he photographed military emplacements until he was finally caught by an observant soldier.

Or this: An old crone limped to her cottage from her daily marketing. In reality she was transmitting via wireless to coordinate insurgents.

Or even this: A police vehicle sped past checkpoints in urgent pursuit of a criminal. The reality was that they were helping three terrorists in their 'police car' escape.

And lastly, a translator and a secret policeman helped three senior insurgents elude their interrogators. Iraq, 2006? No, France, 1943.

So are the "terrorists" who were then British agents and today's insurgents different? The point is each of these stories has a parallel in modern day Afghanistan and Iraq.

Marines landing on the shores of Tripoli did not have CNN waiting for them; Marines today must deal with Al-Jazeera, CBS, NBC and a host of others. Nor were inquiring newsmen searching for emails which might tell where D-Day would happen.

The world is not like that anymore; interest follows news, and news is where you find it. We all remember Geraldo Rivera on live television sketching in sand the attack plan of the company he was embedded with. It became a secret to all but several million viewers. Would you call Geraldo an adversary? Could he get you killed by such antics?

Nothing is as it seems. Insurgency is a thinking man's war. Information Operations is enhanced by the healthy paranoia generated with OPSEC awareness.

Wendell Steavenson, a Western reporter living in Baghdad, said this about a young Iraqi he had interviewed:

Osama's brother Duraid lived with his cousins nearby and sold cans of Pepsi out of Styrofoam coolers just outside the base's concrete blast walls. He came up smiling and gave Sergeant Davis a fist- to- fist handshake. "Hey, you are my brother, man."

We know just about everyone here," said Sergeant Davis, easy, smiling. I smiled back. Then I winced at the things Sergeant Davis did not know; that Duraid had a brother in the resistance and that Duraid himself had fired RPGs at Humvees in Baghdad for the Hell of it.

Steavenson was describing the enemy, only our side didn't know they were the enemy. Is this anything new? During the Vietnam War an American Quaker woman, working as a linguist and health worker with the Vietnamese, had this to say:

Later that afternoon, I swung by the American army compound to pick up the mail, entering the base as the Vietnamese cleaning women left it. I'd often chatted with these women and knew that many of them lived near the My Lai Road. The maids flirted unabashedly as the M.P.s checked their empty baskets for contraband. What fools those M.P.s are, I thought. Doesn't it occur to them that the contraband these women carry is information hidden inside their heads? Do the M.P.s realize that their flirtatious cleaning maids probably pace off warehouse measurements while they sweep, memorize shipments they unload, and note details of any unusual activity? In the years since, I've checked out my guesses, and learned that I was right. Women formed the core of the North Vietnamese/Viet Cong spy, liaison, and distribution networks. Basket by yoked basket, women slipped supplies into locations dangerously close to American bases. Mental picture by mental picture, overheard conversation by overheard conversation; they absorbed information about the enemy and carried it away.

In the museum at Ft. Bragg you can see a perfectly executed map of the interior of a Special Forces base camp, drawn by a 12 year old seamstress. One of my favorite pictures, taken shortly after the conventional Army's victory drive on Baghdad in 2003, shows numerous Iraqis hard at work on an American base. See my point?

Try this test. Find some old magazines. Look at the translators for the American forces in Iraq. In 2003 the translators are wearing street clothes. A year later they all have flak jackets, some helmets. Now none of them goes anywhere without a complete face mask. They have figured out who the enemy is. Have we?

But what if your translator is also out to get you? Since few Americans speak Arabic or Kurdish, who can say what the Iraqis are communicating? One of our jobs is to move, shoot, and communicate, and we can't even ask for the time of day in the language of the people in whose land we find ourselves. A major, recently returned, complained that his translator went to "Arabic secure" when on the phone with a friend. He wondered what the Arab was saying. Was he really on our side? Who were his brothers, his cousins, his sisters? What is his story, what are his resentments, his dreams? Why is he working for us? We must be able to see the world through the eyes of the adversary, the better to know who our enemy is.

We know nothing about the enemy, whom we invite to be among us, because we don't understand whom we can trust. We don't understand because we can't speak to them, but need them to speak for us. We can't convey what is important to us, because we have to go through those intermediaries who might, or might not, convey what we believe to be important. Consider the case of Noureddine Malki. A naturalized citizen, he spied against us when as a translator he passed classified information to Sunni sheiks at the height of combat in Iraq. No one could have known he was a potential spy, because no one adequately researched the lies he told on his applications for citizenship and later his clearance.

Why can't our Army get American linguists? What were our guys doing in Kuwait for the twelve years between Gulf War 1 and the current war? Twelve years seems a long time. Someone could have become a very competent linguist, given the incentive. Had we been there twelve years, or one year, twelve times?

In Iraq, a Marine sniper team was placed on a top floor in a bandit-heavy neighborhood. Suddenly, all action stopped. For two days there was no action. Then the mystery was solved. A Marine saw something taped on the door leading into the team's location in the building. On a piece of masking tape, written in magic marker, a message in Arabic read, "Attention! There's an ambush with American snipers inside this building!"

If you don't know what the sign says, what your translator is saying, what the local radio says, you don't know what is going on. Who is your translator loyal to? You, who will be gone in several months? Or, will your translator perhaps respond to the guy who left a severed head on his mother's doorstep? Or is your translator, as one case study revealed, someone who needs the money and is tired because he has been out every night setting IEDs?

Do you think he would consider it beyond his duties to carry explosives onto your base? Do you check him as he comes into your 'secure' area? Don't you wish your translator was an American?

Who else is out to get us? Some foreigners are, ok. We expected that. But remember, the worst danger is from our own inattention. Our helicopters, our convoys, our patrols are ambushed because we repeat over and over again what we did before. Even the least swift among the bad guys can sit and wait for the next GI's to come be-bopping along on a known path. Of course, the insurgents have also learned to let their Improvised Explosive Devices (IEDs) do their talking, while their bodies are far away. We just die, because we won't change. Go back to Step One.

Step Three: Identify Your Vulnerabilities
Answer: Everything is vulnerable if you let it be so.

Your shirt is not armor. Knowing this, you should do what you can to make yourself less vulnerable. Also knowing this, the adversary (remember, that is either bad people, or good people who are lazy or inattentive…both will kill you) will try everything to take advantage of your vulnerabilities. Know that anything can threaten you. The Commander of the Northern Alliance, Ahmad Shah Masoud, was killed when pretend cameramen set off a bomb made to look like a camera during a phony "interview".

IEDs were first hidden in trash piles on the side of the road, then in dead animals, then in the road, then under the road, then two set to go off separately, and on and on and on, each more sophisticated and deadlier than the last. This happened in every insurgency in modern times. We made it easy for the enemy to blow us up when our patrols left at the same time, in the same configurations, or told the enemy ahead of time during unprotected chatter in the dining facility. In Pakistan, the US Embassy posted their shuttle van's schedule in the lobby. The Americans were ambushed at a van pick up stop. Only the dead brought about a change.

Are you too good to pick up your own trash, do your own laundry, and cut each other's hair? Are you vulnerable when you let others do that, others who are 'on our side'?

Most military personnel know the 'big ground, little round' theory. This concept holds that bullets are tiny in the big wide world, and the chances of them hitting you are slim at best. The "Healthy Paranoia" concept contends differently. It says if you make it easy for an adversary to kill you by your routines or inattentive practices, you will make the little round no longer your distant friend, but your personal death-messenger. If you give away your unit's limitations (such as an email home when you mention that your Humvees haven't been up-armored), or capabilities (when you mention in the dining facili-ty that you have a new night vision device), or countermeasures ("Did you know that the cameras on the gate aren't real, but made to LOOK real?"), it is quite possible you will die, and others as well. You never know who is listening. Ask yourself this next time your cleaning lady comes through. Do you even notice? What is her name?

Step Four: What risks will I take now that I know what the vulnerabilities are?

Answer: Only those that you must which will still allow you to do your job.

'Would you tell me, please, which way I ought to go from here?'

'That depends a good deal on where you want to get to,' said the Cat.

`I don't much care where--' said Alice.

`Then it doesn't matter which way you go,' said the Cat.

`--so long as I get SOMEWHERE,' Alice added as an explanation.

`Oh, you're sure to do that,' said the Cat, `if you only walk long enough.'

Even the dimmest among us know it is important to know what we are supposed to do. Armed with this intelligence, we can plan information operations accordingly. We can employ OPSEC. If I am to take the Commander around to visit the troops, then even I can plan to do so at different times, by different routes. Use movie cameras to film a patrol route. Review it like you would a pre-game show next time you must go into the area... although not by the same route. If a vehicle breaks down, leave a guard on it until we can move it. When we are away, bombers come and plant calling cards. Who has personal cameras in your unit? What are they doing with them? Remember, everyone is out to get you, and you don't want to give the enemy a heads up with Corporal Tent peg's photomontage posted to his personal website after each patrol. The bad guys like to surf the web, too. Who reviews all that goes on the air or online, anyway? Is there ANY control over emails, over web pages, or phone calls to mom?

Step Five: What countermeasures do you employ?
Answer: Whatever ensures the continuation of Step One, above, that is, whatever keeps you and your comrades alive.

You are now sufficiently paranoid to plan appropriately. Everyone is out to get you. Even your friends who are inattentive or too lazy to be alert are out to get you. Your vulnerability is that you are alive in a war zone. Yossarian, the protagonist of Catch 22, realized this. At this point he walked around backwards, naked, with a pistol. He thought, "The enemy is anybody who's going to get you killed, no matter which side he's on... And don't you forget that, because the longer you remember it, the longer you might live." You should think the same way. Of course, you know that already. That is the real reason why basic trainees carry their weapon with them everywhere. This way, being paranoid in a healthy way becomes second nature. This way, you will be prepared; you will stay alive. Remember an old adage from a World War II poster:

A wise old owl sat on an oak.
The more he listened, the less he spoke.
The less he spoke, the more he heard.
Soldier, be like that wise old bird.

Never-ending War

My dad's best friend Eddie, from Navy days in the Second World War, joined the Marines to fight in Korea. War always begins on the grand level. The North Korean invasion of June 1950 was a direct violation of the 1947 United Nations decree. This decree separated the two Koreas at the 38th parallel between US and Soviet occupation zones. Thus the UN mandate for military deployment to Korea was specific: to enforce the restoration of the status quo *ante bellum*. The Security Council voted this resolution while the Soviet Union was absent. With the American military holding on tenuously in Pusan, the United Nations counterattack at Inchon was dramatic, and the victory invigorating. The North Koreans, cut off from their supply routes, retreated in disarray. Then the UN, with the invaders on the run, pursued them deeper into the Communist zone. Combat with the Chinese army came about as the UN military approached the Yalu River. After much fighting, combat stabilized at roughly the same parallel from which it began.

Unlike before, there was no massive outpouring of popular American support for a war far away against a Korean people we knew little about nor understood. Indeed, like all wars, it finally came to an end, but not for Eddie's family. His last letter home, after an arduous journey and a long time lag, spoke of how 'There are more Chinese than we have bullets!' And then there was nothing. Only months later, pieces of news came back to his wife in Iowa. He was first listed as missing in action, and later presumed killed. One of the Chinese human wave attacks finally overwhelmed his Marine detachment. He had a son, also named Eddie, who was almost my age. We met once when we stopped by his mom's home enroute to my cousins in Minnesota. Of course, Eddie's father wasn't there. He never came home. He is gone, somewhere a world away, on a battlefield no one knows. He remains lost to this day. For some of us, wars never end.

A Road With No Signs

The post-Cold War world had no clear orientation markers. Conflicts, such as were previously constrained by great powers' interests, now broke out in remote regions with no one to intervene. What was also different was the advent of television, which brought great human misery into the homes of the West. Moral outrage grew.

In the former Yugoslavia, ethnic and religious conflict broke out once the dominance of a strong communist central government failed. It is instructive to follow the evolution of the United Nations mission in Bosnia. This is an example of post-Cold War change. It is important to know this because people's lives, our family's lives and those of other real people, would be changed forever as a result. My friend told me a horrifying story from his time in Sarajevo, but it is only one of many.

Television stations carried nightly horrors of the Balkans in 1992. Concentration camps discovered with emaciated, tortured people painfully reminded the West of the oft-repeated slogan 'Never Again' with regard to the earlier Holocaust of World War II. Western nations were pressured to do something. Americans, Europeans, and also the Russians discussed what could be done to end the worst slaughter on the continent since the Second World War. No nation wanted to commit their own soldiers or risk a lengthy occupation in embroiled, slaughter-ridden Bosnia.

The UN deployed in 1992. No veto was exercised by any of the Security Council nations. Indeed, a hallmark of post-Cold War UN activities was the lack of such vetoes. Without national interests at stake, but using the UN as a form of concerted 'action', the nations were able to act while not committing large numbers of their own soldiers. They could, however, coordinate ill-defined missions which might require casualties and lengthy occupations. Thus the dramatic drop in the use of the veto, for since the end of the Cold War only seven had been cast.

The Bosnian deployment, known as the UN Protection Force, was initially sent in "to create conditions for peace," whatever that meant. This was later clarified to have UN forces create three demilitarized zones in Croatia. To unclear 'monitoring functions' were added the missions of controlling the populations, observing the Serbian/Croatian cease-fire, then humanitarian assistance. Additionally the mission of enforcing 'no-fly' zones and de-mining were added. The mandate was even expanded to include the creation of 'safe havens'.

Clearly, there was no precedent for how to respond to a civil war that had its roots in deep, historical, ethnic, and religious divisions. The collapse of the central government in Belgrade caused massive refugee flows and social disintegration. Weaponry, which during the Cold War was monitored like a spigot by the great powers, was abundant and little controlled in its aftermath. It overflowed in the looted armories of the former Yugoslavia. The combatant factions themselves had no interest in the cease-fire, when violating it would gain an advantage. The UN troops could only fire in self-defense. UN soldiers were utterly emasculated, caught in the middle, unauthorized to act. When confronted by warring factions shooting each other, the UN could do virtually nothing. Their inability to fight unless fired upon created a self-imposed Achilles Heel. For example, Dutch soldiers in Srebrenica in Bosnia, holding a strongpoint outside an identified "protected Moslem safe haven", found themselves confronted by a Serbian tank. The Serbs pointed their main 122 mm main battle gun at them from only a few feet away. They ordered the Dutch to surrender their weapons, uniforms, and then depart. The Dutch, having no clear rules of engagement against such a blatant act, surrendered and departed. The protected area, one writer noted, thus became a human corral. The UN mission we watched each night was a televised disaster; the nations who voted their presence in Bosnia were forced to act.

Committed to a peace that did not exist, the UN ultimately threatened the Serbs with air strikes if they did not cease actions against the Croats and Muslims. In response, the Serbs employed the expedient of capturing and chaining UN observers to Serb heavy weaponry. In frustration, the West wrung its collective hands. Those with eyes saw this could not continue.

Bizarre incidents occurred. For example, my colleague observed, French soldiers drove in closed armored cars rather than shoot back at a single sniper who killed with impunity anyone walking the streets of Sarajevo. Finally, when NATO entered and changed the rules of engagement (from 'blue' helmets to 'green') the sniper was shot 36 times. Asked why the sniper was shot so often, a French soldier replied, "We ran out of ammunition."

US General John Shalikashvili operated under a changed UN mandate. It allowed enforcement personnel to fire when it appeared there could be a threat. There was no functioning ceasefire until NATO firepower backed it up. This NATO action, however, clearly compromised the actuality of UN neutrality. Yet, it still did not make clear what exactly the UN was trying to accomplish. Clearly, the lack of a clear mission and the absence of a genuine cease-fire created an untenable situation. With their long-cherished impartiality questioned, the UN found itself in a new, dangerous position indeed.

My friend recalls that as part of the 'peacekeeping measures,' Moslem heavy weapons were taken from them. To compensate the Moslems, UN nations committed to future air strikes which would bomb Serbian targets if need be. Such a plan, as we've seen, rendered problematic UN impartiality; since that was still the ostensible role of the UN presence. It was thus only after the massacre of Muslim men and boys in Srebrenica by Serbs, and the world's shocked response, that the UN employed NATO firepower, and blatant combat ceased.

The embattled NATO/UN mission did not, however, resolve the humanitarian crimes that had prompted its' presence in the first place. Horrific facts emerged. War criminals wandered freely within their respective zones since no one wanted to upset the semblance of peace. UN failures in Bosnia grew as their mission expanded.

While Bosnia festered, no limitation seemed to preclude UN deployment. Famine in Somalia, featured nightly on television in the West, caused yet another deployment in 1993. Here too, mission-creep finally ended with UN elements hunting down Farrah Aideed, a local warlord. The clear choosing of sides in a fratricidal war led ultimately to ignominious withdrawal. This deployment evolved, as did Bosnia, into a quagmire with no guidelines for action.

We sometimes ask our military, our sons and daughters, to deploy to places where there is no clear objective. We send them with no answer to the question what victory looks like, or how we propose to achieve it. When we fail to make such matters clear, we as a nation have failed them. Giving guidance is the least we can do for those who've asked to do something for their country. Or, we can do nothing and wait for the next disaster.

A colleague showed me pictures from his deployment to Sarajevo. One photograph showed white fields on a distant hillside above the city. This struck my attention. "I thought you went in summer," I commented. "That looks like snow on the hills".

"No," he replied. "Tombstones."

PART III: WAR AND ILLUSIONS

The Art of war is simple enough. First find out where your enemy is.-- General Ulysses Simpson Grant, ***On the Art of War.***

"Instead of four hundred thousand companions who had fought so many successful battles with them, who had rushed so valiantly into Russia, they saw issuing from the white, ice-bound desert only one thousand foot soldiers and troopers still armed, nine cannon, and twenty thousand beings clothed in rags, with bowed heads, dull eyes, ashy cadaverous faces and long, ice-stiffened beards. Some were fighting for the right to cross the bridge which was still too narrow to accommodate their precipitous flight. Others had rushed down the bank and were struggling across the river, crawling from one jagged cake of ice to another. And this was the Grande Armée!"

ONCE AND FUTURE PRINCIPLES OF WAR

Count Philippe de Ségur, aide-de-camp to Napoleon Bonaparte, thus described the utter rout and blind flight of the haunted remainder of the Grande Armée which had invaded Russia in 1812. As this desperate human wreckage heaved westward from Moscow, a Prussian general staff officer, Count Karl von Clausewitz, was intensely at work in his office on a manuscript to codify the era's "Principles of War.

Tragically, those very principles had been followed carefully by Napoleon's Grande Armée, the same army slaughtered by embattled peasants and fierce Cossacks with little or no military learning. What could have caused this? Without his realizing it, the Man of Destiny, victor of the Pyramids, of Jena, of Austerlitz, the man who swept from the field the flower of enemy soldiery, missed a beat of history. The rules of warfare had changed.

Our nation today sends military personnel around the world. We too have principles of war distilled from ages past. They are mass, objective, offensive, surprise, deception, security, economy of force, unity of command, and simplicity. These principles codify what history suggests should ensure victory in battle against conventional enemies. Simply said, our infantry can close with and destroy the enemy by means of fire and maneuver. Our Navy, as became the norm in the

Spanish-American War, will outgun any enemy vessel. Our aircraft are the finest aerial technology can devise. Are these the principles which will lead to victory today?

A question hovers over this formula, however. Will these principles alone assure victory in our modern engagements, which occur far beyond the battlefield? Do routine shootings during Bosnian humanitarian efforts, roadside bomb explosions in Iraq, kidnapped peacekeepers and murdered soldiers - the standard fare of modern combat - demand additional principles?

What does victory look like today? If today's principles are valid for conventional combat, will they still serve us? Principles are not principles without overall validity; we intuitively know this. A soldier in Vietnam asked, "How do you win an Austerlitz against four people?" Something new is afoot when today's infantryman says he wasn't trained as a street cop. Clearly something unprecedented is happening, or is it just new to our way of thinking? When a young woman straps a bomb to her body to kill our soldiers, or fishermen our sailors, we must ask if our principles retain their validity. How best to determine what principles we need today, if the goal of any such list is victory?

As Machiavelli advised, we may learn whether today's principles still serve us in the light of history. In 1812, motivated by new republican notions of liberty, and Napoleon's desire to defeat the Russian army in order to put pressure on the British to make peace with France, the *Grande Armée*, nearly half of which was composed of soldiers from French allies, invaded Russia and marched towards Moscow, seeking to engage – and defeat – the Russian army in the field. Frustratingly for Napoleon, Russian Marshal Prince Mikhail I. Kutuzov retreated without a fight, drawing the conqueror's regiments behind him.

Forgotten by Napoleon as he charged toward Moscow, or perhaps never known, was another set of war principles written some two millennia earlier by Chinese military scholar Sun Tzu, "The worst policy is to attack cities." Gathering dust, unread, in a former French Royal Military Academy in Paris was the first (1772) translation of Sun Tzu's *Art of War*. These older, little understood, set of principles may serve as a touchstone as we study the changes we are experiencing in our combat today. We cannot hold on to known principles alone if the bitterness of defeat awaits us. Let us see if other principles are helpful.

When at last Marshal Kutuzov was forced by the Czar to fight Napoleon at Borodino, a Homeric slaughter ensued. The Czar's army was drained white by drilled, competent French soldiers who at last engaged the Russians as they stood and fought by known principles. Exhausted, Kutuzov retreated again, with a reinvigorated Napoleon hot on his heels, chafing for the finishing blow. It was getting colder. As Kutuzov fled around Moscow to the distant wastes beyond, Napoleon finally captured the capital and found it... abandoned. The whole city was empty of people, and winter loomed. Here, where should have been triumph and the enemy's surrender, Napoleon discovered his entire army without supplies, food, equipment, and soon, lodging. The Russians actually set fire to areas of the city! This was pure surprise on the battlefield, the greatest fear of any commander. Not only was Napoleon surprised, he didn't even know the city was the 'battlefield'!

After a few more weeks spent in futile pursuit of the elusive Kutuzov, Napoleon abandoned Moscow, and marched back through the howling Russian winter. Kutuzov waited. He waited until his adversary's men lost first their morale to cold and deprivation, then their discipline as ruthlessly they sought everywhere for food, then their unit coherence to sniping Cossack horsemen and enraged peasants whose lands were despoiled, food stolen and homes taken by starving, freezing French soldiers.

Sun Tzu foresaw this when he said, "Do not put a premium on killing. If an army is deprived of its morale, its general will also lose heart. For to win one hundred victories in one hundred battles is not the acme of skill. To subdue the enemy without fighting is the acme of skill. The supreme excellence in war is to attack the enemy's plans." (I wonder if the US Army's 'body count' statisticians ever read this?)

As proven by his strategic retreat toward Moscow, Kutuzov did as Sun Tzu counseled, to "adopt all kinds of measures of deception to drive the enemy into the plight of making erroneous judgments and taking erroneous actions, thus depriving him of his superiority and initiative." Kutuzov became as something 'formless', or as Mao Tse Tung would later say, an "illusion'. One can't strike a devastating blow at an illusion. Stalin traded space for time, and initiated guerrilla war, as Hitler plunged into the vast Soviet steppes during the Second World War. We experienced this in Vietnam. Arguably Saddam Hussein, who read Stalin, did this to us in the Iraqi War of 2003.

Does modern war demand additional principles? Consider. Quarter is not given by para-nations, terrorists, and ethnic groupings which seek to annihilate their enemies. But even a terrorist's war is governed by cool heads. Today's 'warfare' is not open combat so much as guerrilla in nature; thus to understand and fight accordingly would serve us well. America cannot be defeated conventionally, but do we know how to fight an unseen enemy? We have a bounty of precedents to learn from, which are applicable to all combat on the battlefield, and off.

Situational Awareness

General Braddock arrived in America in 1755 to command the British forces sent to subdue the French and their Indian allies at Ft. Duquesne. His senior colonial advisor, the Virginian George Washington, experienced in forest combat, counseled a new type of warfare. Braddock, he recommended, should scout, deploy irregularly, use Indian allies and fight from behind trees. Braddock snubbed these 'unprofessional' notions. The ensuing great slaughter of the English regiments by elusive Indians and animal-skin garbed Frenchmen came as a tremendous shock to British professional soldiers.

The guns of Singapore faced the danger from the sea, but were captured in place by Japanese soldiers who, the British defenders contended, could never cross the Malay Peninsula. Likewise in Vietnam, the French in their valley fortress of Dien Bien Phu were overrun by thousands of Vietminh who pounded their enemies with cannon they 'could not possibly' transport to such a remote district, as US Army professionals concurred. Few are aware that modest Afghani girls fled in fear from Americans because they were told that GIs with sunglasses could see through their dresses.

Situational Awareness is something that which encompasses more than knowing your enemy's combat strength. It requires knowing his morale, his beliefs, and his imagination. At most, the best- prepared soldier would study the language of his adversary, thus to understand his mind, and read his plans. If we can speak to our enemy, we will not be dependent upon translators who know more about us than we do about them; whose relatives are unknown and allegiances are dubious. At least, our military principle should examine the logistics, history, capabilities and characteristics of an adversary; how they fought in the past, why they fight, and how they might imaginatively be engaged.

The hallmark of this principle is adaptability. Using intelligence about the enemy, our responses may vary, become unpredictable. Mao Tse Tung wrote, "Containing forces may be turned into assault forces, and (vice versa)."

Subsumed in all this is deception and surprise, for isn't victory the ultimate goal of adapting to concrete conditions?

Proportionality

With the advent of our war against terrorists, many have argued for getting rid of boundaries. No Geneva Convention, no Hague trials. Even the use of torture has been seriously considered. Is this what will win? A Special Forces combat veteran recalled a tasking to suppress an enemy artillery position. "The Rangers proposed an insertion, then, by fire and maneuver, to overrun the place. Limited casualties, mission accomplished. I asked, 'Why not insert a single man with a high-powered rifle and a layout of the compound? With a few well-aimed shots he could destroy the position's only communications gear. Mission accomplished." Sun Tzu would have agreed, because the aim of war is not killing, it is not even war, it is victory. The goal is to win without having to fight, or if fighting, to do only that which allows one to win. This is because the battle only ends the physical combat; it does not win the peace.

Consider the advent of the media's presence, and thus of the smart bomb. This is a weapon of democratic nations which must answer to public opinion. Not so with dictatorships or guerrillas. The Soviets would demolish whole city blocks in their counterattack on Germany, or during their 1956 invasion of Hungary, if the least resistance emanated from a single window. Not so the French in Algeria in 1962 when General Massou employed torture against the 'Liberation Organization'. The French press howled that they leave the field!

Sun Tzu said it best, "Generally in war it is best to take a state intact; to ruin it is inferior to this." Measured applications of force and discussion are equally appropriate, depending on the circumstances. Americans tend to admire the fighter but do not as often recognize the victor who gained his accomplishment through wit. It was also true in Sun Tzu's time, "When you subdue your enemy without fighting, who will pronounce you valorous?"

Napoleon cost the lives of untold thousands, but who remembers French General Hubert Lyautey, arguably the most successful colonial soldier? In the early 1900's, incredibly, he sought fewer, not more Frenchmen on the ground in Algeria. He 'deployed' a clever array of liaisons with local chieftains, based on superior intelligence, disciplined soldiers, wise proclamations, and honest dealings with the locals whom he enlisted in his cause.

Discipline

Wisdom, Credibility, Benevolence, Courage, and Discipline--the Five Qualities of a Good General, Chinese Wisdom

Frustration is the feeling of the professional soldier who battles the guerrilla. The guerrilla hides in the sea of people. When the occupying soldier perceives the population of the country as a potential enemy, he is never at rest; he never experiences a moment of true peace. John Steinbeck in his 1942 novel *The Moon is Down* revealed this sense of the occupier's utter despair about dealing with a hostile public. "You know what (the orders) are, 'Take the leaders, shoot the leaders. Take hostages, shoot the hostages, take more hostages, shoot them', and his voice had risen but now it sank almost to a whisper, 'and the hatred keeps growing and the hurt between us keeps growing deeper and deeper.' "

Later in the story another officer would say, "We are like flies. We are like flies that have captured two hundred miles of flypaper."

The guerrilla knows this and exploits it. Bizarre practices such as beheading Westerners as in Iraq, or skinning Soviets alive as in Afghanistan, or suicide bombings, or simple torture of captured soldiers are calculated by guerrilla leaders to provoke the frustrated military to violate their own standards of moral behavior, seek revenge, and commit atrocities, as at My Lai. Atrocities produce new guerrillas, new atrocities, as the cycle of revenge whirls.

In John Steinbeck's The Moon is Down, the German commander in occupied Norway, who lived through the First World War, commented on an earlier occupation, "I remember a little old woman in Brussels... We didn't know her son had been executed. When we finally shot her, she had killed twelve (of our) men with a long black hatpin." "But you shot her, and the murders stopped?" "No, they did not stop. When we finally retreated, they cut off the stragglers, and burned some and gouged out the eyes of others. Some they even crucified."

Atrocities create disgust at home, outrage in the media, and shame among the soldiery. Atrocities deepen frustration as it becomes clear that such violations don't stop the guerrillas, but actually encourage them. The professional soldier's frustration is exploited by a disciplined insurgent force and serves the guerrilla's purpose without his having to fire a shot. As Sun Tzu observed, "before he has bloodied his blade, his enemy...has already submitted."

Atrocity and abuse stories, repeated over and over among the populace, hurt the occupier more than those whom such actions were intended to intimidate.

Thus, discipline and leadership among professional soldiers are paramount to protect against provocation and propaganda. Any slip in discipline literally serves the enemy, who can communicate such a shortfall in any way he wants. In this sense, all warfare is deception, for it is how the message is conveyed that wins. As against provocation and propaganda, so must our principle govern how we respond. "One who wishes to simulate cowardice and lie in wait for the enemy must be courageous, for only then is he able to simulate fear. One who wishes to appear to be weak in order to make his enemy arrogant must be extremely strong."

These concepts are not common to our military. Only disciplined soldiers can withstand temptations, as when starving US soldiers at Bastogne were lured to surrender, tempted by German loudspeakers promising "a gourmet dinner tonight and here is the menu..."

To paraphrase Sun Tzu, if we know the enemy, and know ourselves, we will not lose.

Patience

Americans are the most impatient people in the world. We pride ourselves on this because it represents initiative, decisiveness, and action. Such a trait, unbalanced by wise patience where appropriate, can cost lives. As Sun Tzu argued, and Mao Tse Tung paraphrased, "We do not allow any of our Red Army commanders to become rash and reckless hot heads. (We) must encourage every one of them to become a hero, brave and wise, with not only courage to overcome obstacles but the ability to control changes and developments."

Consider the wisdom of tactically sending soldiers out on patrol, or on recon boats up rivers, to 'draw fire'. Is this the offensive? Is this initiative? It appears it is action to no particular end. Why would preemption be preferable to defeating the enemy by design? Recall that Sun Tzu said the excellent goal is to defeat the enemy's strategy, then to break his alliances, and only then, once victory cannot be won without a shot fired, his army. "Do not allow your enemies to get together... Look into the matter of his alliances and cause them to be severed and dissolved. If an enemy has alliances, the problem is grave and the enemy's position strong; if he has no alliances the problem is minor and the enemy's position weak."

There is nothing worse than being in a strange country, unable to see the enemy, who wants you to feel so very alone. Waiting is not delay for delay's sake if the 'battle' is later won. If connivance or negotiation can defeat the enemy's plans, break up his alliances, and cause him to disband his war effort, is that not victory? If patience saves our people's lives, then the wait was more valuable than a pretended decisiveness. Impetuous action is perhaps worst because without considering beyond the combat phase of the war, the ensuing peace may be even worse.

Once all methods of destroying an enemy's strategy, his alliances, and ability to fight are tried, be it by diplomacy, a coup, by the well-aimed shot, or by winning the people to our side, then we might reconsider our means. Often we can win without having to fire a shot. As Abraham Lincoln said, "If I make my enemy my friend, haven't I destroyed him?" We only need to know what victory looks like.

Prudence

The movie Karate Kid said it best. "What is the best way to avoid a punch?" the youth asked. The wise man paused a moment, then said, "The best way to avoid a punch is, don't be there." We Americans like direct action. We don't like something we don't control and that doesn't have a clear outcome. We are poor combatants when it comes to protracted war. Our enemies know we can't stand an endless game without result. Football is our sport where you march according to rules down the gridiron, and the game is over when the clock runs out. Few Americans play chess; the open-ended conflict is not in our nature. We prefer overwhelming firepower. We cannot fathom the patience of the weak foe who knows that victory comes only when we are worn down, not driven from the field. Napoleon's army was beaten by an ill-trained, poorly-used Slavic soldiery despite his having the best- educated, most carefully trained and combat-experienced officers in the world. What happened? What did it mean that an army, wholly schooled in military training and on the invaluable field of battle, could be so completely destroyed?

Count de Ségur observed that had Napoleon not tried to defeat countless serfs on their homeland, but rather enflamed the Russian hearts with the prospect of liberty, he could have won. He would have completely triumphed, perhaps not have had to fight at all. He could have allowed the serfs to throw out their masters with material support from the Grande Armée!

Instead, Napoleon drove for symbolic Moscow.

Again, Sun Tzu, "they entice him with something he is certain to take, and with lures of ostensible profit they await him in strength."

Napoleon did not have the prudence to detect such a ploy. He lost heart; his army fled the field, and dissolved into history without the Russians firing a shot.

Conclusion

In 1939 a Chinese military strategist named Guo Huaruo prepared Sun Tzu's writings and distributed them in Chinese Communist-controlled areas. Mao Tse Tung read them carefully. He took the lessons to heart, and conquered China. The principles distilled here, situational awareness, proportion, discipline, patience, prudence, are not new. They are, however, universal and will require training to prevail in modern conflicts.

In 1774, British statesman Edmund Burke advised Parliament that war with America could be avoided, and friendship maintained, through conciliation. "The use of force alone is but temporary. It may subdue for the moment; but it does not remove the necessity of subduing again: and a nation is not governed, which is perpetually to be conquered."

Our duty is to protect the lives of those entrusted to us. Better to win through wisdom, or if forced, with proportion that wins the peace. Better to include these age- old principles with what we now practice. We should all live to enjoy life, liberty, and the pursuit of happiness; we're all in this together.

Our Army's Good Legacy Abroad

A sepia photograph from the 1890's shows men playing a sport on the parade ground of an old Army cavalry post. No one wore a glove like we would recognize today, but they were clearly arranged around a field with a determined batter getting ready to slug a baseball. It occurred to me that these soldiers of yesteryear were distant ambassadors of the kind of people we believe ourselves to be today.

We need only recall our presence throughout Mexico and the Caribbean during the first half of the Twentieth Century. In those long-ago outposts as far flung as Puerto Rico, the Sonoran Desert, the Dominican Republic, Nicaragua, and Cuba, our soldiers might have left little impact. One lasting, joyful, result of their presence, however, cannot be denied: they left the local people with the love of baseball. Today's American and National League baseball stars from across the Gulf of Mexico and Lesser Antilles can be traced directly to amateur sportsmen who wore uniforms of the United States. Indeed, many of the famous players of the early Negro Leagues were soldiers who once played on Ft. Huachuca's team in Arizona. Their role abroad is memorialized in countless ad hoc baseball fields wherever US Army soldiers were sent.

Most think we are represented overseas by dignitaries in suits who work in embassies. Yet, if we meet average people from abroad, we find if they've met any American at all, they've more than likely met an American service member. It is from what these average Americans do while abroad that our reputation overseas is often determined. This truism is a facet of our history of which we can be especially proud.

Few military people speak a foreign language. They are sent overseas with little if any briefing on what to expect, how to behave, and what they might do to offend or charm the local population. This is not a new phenomenon. Americans were considered naïve or arrogant long before "*The Ugly American*" was written. One need only remember the scene in that novel where a loud American businessman bellows, 'Get a picture of the priest! Get a picture of the priest!' at the silent height of a sacred Buddhist ceremony. Such a scene causes one to realize what we must overcome about our reputation abroad. Today the military services offer online 'cultural awareness' training. Occasionally an actual person from the local society is invited to give a presentation. It's a start.

Yet consider the unpracticed, genuine goodwill that we bring abroad, which comes from something for which we need little training, in fact no training at all. The average American loves sports. Sports don't need language skills, only a willingness to show another how to play. Our oldest son Marty came home one day from his American Department of Defense grade school in the Netherlands. He asked if we had a basketball. He said he'd walked by a place where a lot of African kids were sitting around a basketball goal doing nothing. "They acted like they didn't know what to do," Marty observed. "They spoke French, so I asked them why they didn't play basketball. They'd never heard of it." This strange story was worth investigating. It turned out that the young Africans were refugees from West Africa, thus the French language. Yet they were left at the refugee center to their own devices most of the day, awaiting the long immigration procedure. We know now, if we know nothing more about them, that some American took the time to show them how to play basketball. It is something they won't forget. In fact, some years later, that ball and the hoop were still in good use by other young players.

Our legacy abroad? We can speak of democracy, the rule of law, and freedom of the press. Yet is that, strictly speaking, our American military legacy? You don't shoot these cultural traits into being. Such legacies come about, if at all, after years of trial and error, after the battles are fought and peace returns. What no one takes away from us is our love of sports such as baseball and basketball. They are simple, and easy to play. They are characterized by sportsmanship, which respects fair play, and a spirited game. They don't require lots of equipment, and there is no language barrier. When the Army was in Puerto Rico after the Spanish-American War in Mexico in 1916, the Marines in Nicaragua and Santo Domingo in the 1930's, or GIs in Japan in the 1940's, Panama in the '90s or Djibouti now, we brought along a baseball. A makeshift Iraqi squad was even invited to play in the Green Zone by Army players! It is a game still obsessively played throughout most of these lands today, although Iraqis fear counterinsurgent hatred as a result. Nevertheless, as American baseball spread in other countries, it proves that in a strange way, sportsmanship always wins out in the end.

The story is always the same. Average American soldiers play on a makeshift field, and someone invites the locals to come play. Talk about bridge building; this is open, genuine, culture sharing! We can be proud of this legacy every time we hear the call to "Play Ball!"

War That Never Ends: Landmines

Anthony Bourdain hosts an exotic food show. He travels the world for delicacies strange and foreign. Once, however, he shared a dinner under circumstances I'll never forget. Bourdain commented, after a most hospitable, simple meal with a Laotian peasant family, that even he, a brash New Yorker, was at a loss for words. His dinner host displayed all the courtesy of a duke, even though he'd lost an arm and a leg to a landmine dropped in some conflict three decades earlier. It didn't matter who might have placed it; the man wasn't even alive when it was placed in its sinister hole. The man's arm and his leg were gone forever.

My family was one of the first to visit the Bohemian countryside after the Iron Curtain fell. Nothing, in my opinion, can match the charm of that fabled region of mysterious woods, sparkling streams, and undulating forested hills. I recall we were walking in the former "No Man's Land" on the Bavarian/Czech border, where machine-gun emplacements, guard towers, and patrol roads had fallen into disuse. Nature was reclaiming an area only previously cleared for avenues of fire. My three sons were bounding around, while my wife and I remarked upon the German gravestones still to be found under the pine trees. No one had lived here for some forty-five years.

Then one of the boys came over to me and said, "Look, Daddy. What are those?"

Clustered at the base of a stream bank were several landmines, eroded away from an area supposedly cleared. I line-marched my family out of there, nature's reverie shocked away by a chilling fear which locked onto our every step. The reality of landmines, forgotten and left there from the recently ended Cold War, seared itself into my mind. The attractive forest path might have enticed my whole family to slaughter.

Once in my travels I came across a strange comic book. It had no words, because it was designed for the illiterate. It told the story of a farm girl who was violated by a land baron. To get revenge, she took the advice of another farmer who showed her how to put a bomb in the ground outside the baron's door. To set the bomb, the rape victim made a trigger out of a lock of her own hair. Of course, the land baron was dramatically blown up. This book, "Mine Warfare", was printed in millions and distributed to the Chinese peasantry by Communist activists in the war against their former government. It was a way poor people could defeat a well-financed military, by using passive devices, which are remarkably deadly.

Later, "Bouncing Betties" from the Vietnam War, blew the leg off one soldier, then propelled a secondary device into the air to kill even more. Then there were 'toe-poppers', which blew off only a part of a foot, causing other soldiers to be rendered combat ineffective while they treated the wounded man. Today, of course, there are roadside bombs which destroy whole vehicles and incinerate those inside.

I recall another mine I left in a field. I'd called in a field exercise airstrike. It was a technological wonder to behold. The bomb fell from the aircraft, and as it plummeted to the ground it opened like a piñata. From inside rained hundreds of bomblets, scattering bursts all across the countryside. The symphony of explosions was greeted with cheers, because the target area was well and truly destroyed. Of course, all the bombs didn't go off. I didn't know that then, but I know it now. In fact, I think about a quotation I read much later in life, when John Woodward Phillip, a US Naval officer in the Spanish-American War, upon seeing the enemy Spanish cruiser Vizcaya in flames, patiently told his men, "Don't cheer boys. The poor devils are dying." The mines I dropped that didn't explode that day are still there for all I know, still awaiting a day they can kill some poor devil. Millions of such mines lay all around the world.

Recently the British government put out for bid a contract to disable the seventy-seven or so minefields left behind in the distant Falklands Islands during the 1982 War of that name. Angola, in Africa, was recently on television, having hired a contractor to train locals to try to find the millions or so of mines left behind from their civil war. An

American sergeant was killed by a mine in Bosnia, when he stepped out of his vehicle to eat under a nearby tree. The stories, indeed, are endless. Those who laid the mines are long gone; the wars long, long over. For whatever reasons they were once placed in the ground, nothing compelled them to be removed. That is because while even American soldiers are trained to "Close with and destroy the enemy by means of fire and maneuver", nothing is said about what that firepower leaves behind. We rained millions of cluster bomblets on Vietnam; the Soviets did the same in Afghanistan. America continues, along with other major industrial nations, to sell such cluster bombs around the world. That is why millions of these bomblets are unaccounted for after combat is over, because they never all go off once a bomb is dropped. Mines are quite literally everywhere, in some fashion or other.

Shells left over from World War I, that's correct, World War I, are found weekly in Belgium and France. They are still dangerous, even today. Belgian explosives experts defuse thousands in what is called the "Iron Harvest". I recall an electric jolt of panic when I saw our friend's toddler son happily brushing away the dirt around a hand grenade left lying on a pathway; it was left over from the Great War.

Of course, those who die from forgotten mines tend to be animals, children, or farmers, in distant lands. Simple prosthetic devices allow those whose legs and arms are blown off to hobble around, the suffering of body and mind lasting forever. Their parents see them, and the pain never ends. Those who continue to create and manufacture these devices are a panoply of technicians, businessmen, military specialists, and others with advanced degrees. Those who employ them are military, liberators, ideologues, visionaries, or other saviors who never see down the road. Perhaps you know some of them.

Then there are those who try to learn how to disable roadside bombs, build mine-detecting robots, and develop mine-identification technologies. These people often work for the same country as made the mines in the first place. The irony is never noted.

Today mine detection in Angola uses a method of sticks tied together in a foot-wide square. The square is laid on the ground, and a knife is prodded inside the marked area to see if something is there. That is about where shared modern technology has brought us. No one knows where most mines are, for neither the peasants nor the fighter bombers left maps. The results of the mines, though, go on and on. Abandoned fertile fields, maimed mothers, their crippled children and their broken menfolk are the never-ending legacy of sowing pods of death.

We in the West could win over whole populations if we set as a goal to develop a mine-detection technology that brought us out of the nineteenth century and that could be shared cheaply, widely, and effectively. Imagine a Nobel Prize for the scientist who saved the lives of even those yet to be born, who cleared mines so the fields would once again bloom with food. Suppose we start somewhere. Regardless of who placed them, the mines are there in their millions worldwide. I never signed up to kill unto future generations anywhere; no one I know did. Yet we have a chance to do something good. Perhaps now, perhaps even now we can do something to save those yet to be killed by a mine. We can influence a scientist, an inventor, a dreamer. Who knows, the same politicians who avoid the Ottawa Treaty to ban anti-personnel mines might at least want to be the ones to introduce a modern detection technology that finds them. They can win the prize that clears minefields once and for all, so families don't tread in fear anymore, and can enjoy a walk in the country.

Questions for a Counterspy

*T*hese questions were posed by Jenny Kile, creator of the website 'Mysterious Writings', to the author. She writes:

In a time of uncertainty and of dangers lurking all around us, John Davis brings a sense of peace. He offers captivating glimpses into his past line of work as a counterintelligence officer, linguist, and federal civil servant in his book, Rainy Street Stories: Reflections on Secret Wars, Espionage, and Terrorism. By understanding there are those working towards harmony, and not through additional violence, I found it illuminating. To learn the minds of others helps us understand better, and helps us to be able to live more safely in the world. Enjoy.

Questions:

1) The hidden and secret wars expressed in your book, Rainy Street Stories, certainly cause one to pause. You share stories from a world, often unknown or unseen, and filled with mystery, intrigue, and danger. A world you once lived in. Your book is an engaging and excellent read. What prompted you, or why was it important for you to write a book on this subject?

I wrote this because I believe it is important for citizens of a free society to know what they are calling upon those of us in the secret world to do. I hoped to put human faces on the consequences of abstract policies, case work, and even historical events. Moreover, I thought few knew the real, ground- level atmosphere of surveillance work or the mysterious demands of secret contacts and missions of such a world.

The questions of loyalty, trust, and betrayal are always present, and I wanted people to be somewhat aware of what it is to live in such a morally problematic condition. As I mentioned in the preface to *Rainy Street Stories*, there is no free pass from right and wrong… even, or especially, in the secret world.

We are a society of laws, and should always remember that what makes us the 'good guys' is how we adhere to the norms of a liberal democracy. It was for this reason that I wrote so vociferously against torture in Rainy Street Stories.

2) *You met people and experienced lifestyles from all across the world. Are your feelings we are much the same, no matter where we live, or do you feel there are great differences causing such covert battles to continually emerge?*

I discovered, once I looked 'around the corner', so to speak, that just like Shakespeare said in Hamlet, "There are more things in heaven and earth, Horatio, than are dreamt of in your philosophy." – Hamlet (1.5.167-8), Hamlet to Horatio.

There are many beliefs, philosophies, and personalities about which we know little. Part of the adventure of life is to learn of, and about, others. We find many similarities of course, but it is the differences which cause us to grow, and perhaps learn something. Our role is to remain open to surprises, and be discerning in what is good, or bad, as we grow in knowledge of what those terms mean. One truism I've discovered is that the more you know of others, the less you fear them. Personally, I've always valued exchange programs between people of different lands, the better to know one another in their actual living conditions. The more we know of others, the safer our world will be.

3) *Reading your book spurs thoughts that maybe the conspiracy theorists know quite a lot. :). It makes me wonder how much control and power comes from a clandestine few. Can you share thoughts on this? Do you feel secret societies, such as the so called illuminati or P2, are instigators to turmoil or peace? How threatening or helpful to us is the world you knew? Should we make ourselves more aware?*

No, I don't subscribe to conspiracy theories which maintain that a knowledgeable few control events. This is not to say over the years such groups haven't tried! As an analyst of human nature, as it is played out in world affairs, I find that chance, pure dumb luck, and surprise play far greater roles than conspiracies. A story that sounded too pat, too neatly tied up with a ribbon, was always suspect to me.

There are traits of human nature which can be understood, however, but these are not easily codified. Secrets don't remain so for long, particularly so long as human beings want to know. And we always want to know. I agree with the conclusions reached many years ago by the Congressional Committee chaired by Senator Daniel Patrick Moynihan when he argued for less, rather than more, secrecy. Too much secrecy threatens a democratic society. We can't remain beholden to only a select few (even if elected) to distill what we as a society are allowed to know. In fact, I'm an advocate for intelligence oversight.

Many avenues should be available within the system for those who question the legality of something. This has been done quite well in many agencies I've worked in. I also believe in a free press. As Moynihan contends, we need to put a limit to what we declare secret, and how long it stays that way, if we are to make informed judgments, or scholars are to write true histories.

Perhaps if we did so, we wouldn't be so surprised by world events! Paradoxical, isn't it? Transparency in government affairs is always, always preferable to secrecy. If only for our own good!

EASTER MORN

On Easter Sunday a bomb killed 72 people at a play park in Lahore, Pakistan.

Blind the brush that swept the children from their games that morn.

Blind the sweep of little ones who from their play were torn.
What manner of dark furies, of hatred's smell so bitter
Could lead to such an end, of boys, and girls, by murder?

Remind me now, how grand the cause, which led the killers there.
Remind me what great goal should maim grandfather in his chair,
Who watched as little voices called with laughter and great joy,
Whose little heart aches were all cured by mommy's nearby voice.

But mother could no longer help, nor father fears allay,
For they too were all murdered on that acrid, doom-wrought day.
Only crying little bodies, little souls now gone away,
Can e'er recall the dawning of this now past Easter Day.

Compromise?

We read about suicide bombs going off... far away. Street markets get blasted by whistling mortar shells. Villages with no running water get overrun, burned to the ground, and all the inhabitants are massacred. Towns in places with unpronounceable names are blown to bits and terrorized by roving gangs of killers. Then ethnic groups are chased away or murdered because, well, they are different.

Do you wonder about our future? We, all of us, want our future to be peaceful. If wars factor into your ideas, you no doubt hope they are elsewhere, very far, far away. Where do wars come from, anyway? Why have we been spared here?

Before you answer this, think. What do we have others don't? We all have a way to feel a part of our country. We can vote. After the vote, there is a change of government, without violence. We feel relatively safe. Few places on earth can say this. This is a safe, relatively fair, country. Where it is not, we can act to change it through reforms.

How did we get to this favored place? One man, Edmund Burke, a great British parliamentarian from the era of our Revolution, said it best to his colleagues, who did not want to compromise with America. "All government, indeed every human benefit and enjoyment, every virtue, and every prudent act, is founded on compromise." Burke wanted to compromise with the rebellious colonials. He wanted them to feel closer to the English Motherland, whose ancient rights they sought to have redressed. He wanted to compromise with them and keep them as part of the British Empire. His British Parliamentary colleagues did not. They wanted no compromise; they wanted to fight the colonies. They fought by sending thousands of their sons to America, and they lost thousands of their young men, killed on American battlefields.

Compromise? When is the last time you heard an American politician say that? For that matter, when was the last time you thought about that? Compromise is what we learned when we found out we couldn't all play on the swing at the same time. We learned to share, and if everyone got a chance at using the ball field, everyone was satisfied. He knew his turn would come.

Now I've seen people talk about other Americans as the enemy. 'They don't agree with me, so I hate them.' Reading some of the unsourced and unidentified commentaries on the Internet, you'd think we were a nation divided against itself. Hating ourselves. The attitude is, "When we get in we'll clean this place up! We are good, and they are evil. There is no middle ground; all good is on our side, and they are less than us." Such a strange mentality sweeps many corners of our land. Such people don't believe in the fundamental purpose of compromise; to preserve our way of government, indeed our way of life.

I read recently how the great 19th Century was believed to be the pinnacle of success. The Industrial Revolution brought untold wealth, speed, literacy, and awareness of fighting previously dread diseases to the great nations of the world. They were proud of all their achievements. Progress, it seemed, would go on forever.

Progress ended with the Great War. World War I showed how far people had really come. They couldn't compromise, and thought their wealth would protect them. They thought the wars would be fought elsewhere, with other people's children. Instead, poison gas, machine guns, high explosives, flame throwers, mines, airplanes, submarines, and hand grenades, all products of this great era of mechanical advancement, slaughtered men by the millions in trenches; trenches where they lived like bugs or rats.

This is what happened when so called civilized people didn't compromise. We think it can't happen here, now. Why?

THE JIHADI WHO LOVED FOOTBALL

A British mother almost mad with grief begs her child who's disappeared to, "Come home. At least let me know you are alive." A French Muslim widow weeps uncontrollably because her only son no longer even sends emails from Syria. She heaves with sorrow. She cannot believe her son, a lonely, troubled seventeen-year-old, could leave his family in Paris, the land where he was born. Americans from New York to Alabama are stunned to realize their children, raised in good circumstances, in often well educated, assimilated households, disappear to join the 'Jihad'.

These are the faces of many Western parents. Their child has become a 'jihadi' who has stolen away to fight for the Islamic State or similar movements. The vanished young people are thoughtful, from all walks of life, but somehow lost. Somehow, some way, this vulnerability was discovered. Someone took the time to 'recruit' them to an apocalyptic, puritanical, yet nevertheless appealing cause.

The Islamic State, for example, gives a young wanderer's life meaning. It challenges them in ways 'a pampered, decadent, meaningless' Western life does not. They are called upon to fight as valiant lions in defense of 'Islamic women who are raped, and children who are murdered'. Rallied by unknown enthusiasts to a fight worth dying for, they leave as international volunteers to battle against 'the butcher Assad regime' in Syria, or the 'apostate Shia government in Iraq' to name but two. The list of arch enemies of true Islam is worldwide. Indeed, a simple review of Islamic State social media indicates remarkably clear guidance. The world is reduced to a simple, easily understood black- and- white. Searchers are counseled they are less than good Muslims if they don't make a decision. 'Act! Don't sit in coffee houses or McDonald's and waste your lives. Fight the noble fight against unbelievers and apostates in Syria and Iraq. After all, to die killing those propped up by Crusaders and Jews leads to Paradise in Heaven. What are you waiting for? What are you doing just sitting in your mom's basement? Be somebody! Defend your true faith and the wretched sufferers of Islam!'

This, of course, is propaganda. Yet it works. How it works is my theme. What Western nations can do to combat it is my proposal. Yet at this juncture, I must add, what we'll discover is that we've known all along about this problem. It appeared in different guises throughout our own recent history.

There is nothing new under the sun. Appeals like this were made to young, idealistic students and workers in the 1930's. Then the battle cry was to 'Fight Fascism' in Spain. 'Why sit at home when the Western Democracies appease the Fascists? These sham democracies won't fight in Spain? Arise workers from your slumber! Go out to fight the bosses, the cops, and the priests in the one place where you can with a gun! If your governments won't arm the workers of Spain, secretly make your own way there. Shoot down the police and army who protect those who've robbed your class since time began! Come to Spain and fight. Your life will be made whole when you show class solidarity. You need only go there to fight with class brothers! A wonderful bond of kinship like you've never known will be yours.'

Imagine the impact of these noble sentiments on young, romantic, resentful students living in rain swept college dorm rooms in London. Or consider these calls to disaffected, quietly enraged working men facing another day, month, and year on the dreary line at the packing plant. Going to Spain, their lives would become, in a word, meaningful.

Such calls to battle in Spain appeared in easily accessible penny periodicals. Shrill posters carried this message under a scene of aerial bombardment, "If you tolerate this, your children will be next!" Rallies accompanied by memorable music such as the emotionally-charged *Jarama* and *No Pasarán* cheered Westerners to fight the 'Fascist rebellion' against the Spanish Republican government. The great author George Orwell was one of the true believers who left England to fight Franco. He came home disillusioned and physically shattered from a bullet in the neck. As recounted in his deeply moving *Homage to Catalonia*, he arrived in Spain to find not battlefield fellowship among like-minded idealists, but rather a death slog between driven, relentless, and bloody-minded foes. He found little military leadership. He discovered his Internationalist comrades were little more than cannon fodder. Slaughtered from one fight to the next, he was astounded to realize that not only the 'Fascists' but his own side was hunting him down. Indeed, the Communists of Stalin's NKVD secret police were cleansing the Republican side of those deemed ideologically impure. Orwell ended his time in Spain pursued through the streets of Barcelona by Stalinist Gestapo-like thugs. Thus evolved Orwell's change of heart, which led to such world- stunning works as *Animal Farm* and *1984*. The man who'd left for what he believed a noble cause found it just another manipulation. He'd been used by cynical, power-driven men. Not for nothing did his cynical character say in 1984:

"The German Nazis and the Russian Communists came very close to us in their methods, but they never had the courage to recognize their own motives. They pretended, perhaps they even believed, that they had seized power unwillingly and for a limited time, and that just around the corner there lay a paradise where human beings would be free and equal. We are not like that. We know that no one ever seizes power with the intention of relinquishing it. Power is not a means; it is an end. One does not establish a dictatorship in order to safeguard a revolution; one makes the revolution in order to establish the dictatorship. The object of persecution is persecution. The object of torture is torture. The object of power is power. Now you begin to understand me."

So too may we understand the current disappearances of young men and women in pursuit of a pure Islamic religion on earth. Consider this a modern nuance to the old theme. Today's jihadist appeals sound for all the world like super-hero comic books of days gone by. Today, jihad is sold as the world's coolest video game... only it is real. The all-virtuous jihadi, who after all believes he is fighting for almighty God, battles against the worldwide lies, wiles, and deceits of totally evil arch enemies. Islamic State videos enhance this by pictures of cool gunfights where jihadists hold rifles over walls and spray ammo until the clip is empty. Bullets flash and evildoers fall, but never the hardy jihadis. They only explode themselves for God after filming stout hearted home-videos to explain why God wants them to do so. Jihadists spin figure eights with tanks, liberate adoring crowds, and make evil incarnate apostates, devil aerial killers, and *kuffars* suffer and pay for their sins. Recruiters know this appeals to the same type of young person who plays hundreds of video games over the years... if not thousands. The secret recruiters know such lonely, misfit young people might one day, in the mall, look at themselves and ask, "What have I done with my life?" Along comes the friendly deceiver, often online, who whispers like Mephistopheles in his ear, "You can have all this, if you only act for God." He speaks of a God who will reward a young, aimless person with all he can imagine. Power, happiness, understanding and... love. Imagine the impact this might have on a lonely, rudderless young person. He might be a barely practicing Muslim who feels he has no future; who feels nothing gives his life a larger purpose than hanging out at the mall or smoking cigarettes. Or, it might appeal to a well-established, career bound Muslim who nevertheless feels an outsider in the Western world. He feels he lives a dual existence. He's never discovered who he really is. He comes to believe he cannot practice his faith properly, for has not the recruiter suggested as much? A recruitment is like making a marriage proposal. The right words are said, the heartfelt appeals rendered; understanding, breathless vows are made, the correct hopes, dreams, and cares are sighed for, before the 'question is popped'. Indeed, studies have shown that poetry plays a large part in celebrating jihad. The longing and loneliness of the believer, his alienation from the truth, and his dreams of perfection in the world to come, are all present in such romances of verse. One recruitment of a Western girl to jihad began by the recruiter sending flowers, then prayer cards, then scarves and even chocolates. No mention was made of jihad until long into the developed relationship. The recruiter who used this method himself now works for the West. He helps turn lost Muslims away from extremism. He explained that a compassionate, available and truly hearing ear, an open heart, and yet a cynical purpose allowed recruiters to succeed over and over. They knew the language young searchers wanted to hear, and the religious quotations which would bring them along when they wavered.

Much is discussed today about what to do about the thousands of Westerners who have gone to 'fight in Syria', or any number of other places, or perhaps even here at home. Many argue they should lose their citizenship. Others say they should be jailed. Some suggest they be shot. Still others suggest a type of 'deprogramming', as if what caused them to leave is a type of computer process which can be reversed if only codes are switched. In successful programs in Antwerp, Belgium, in Canada, and Denmark, social workers help identify possible future jihadis. These projects attempt to connect with young searchers, some as young as ten or twelve. And why should social workers go into grammar schools? Because the recruiters for jihad don't hesitate to reach out there. Muslim communities, in concert with government elements such as schools in different countries, or even alone, can stop recruitment by extremists. Such communities employ former recruiters, converts to their faith, youth leaders and imams to identify and contradict lies being spread to recruit young people to war. They defuse the language of the deceivers, and show God is not about murder, or power, or vengeance. One former recruiter, now fighting extremism, asked vulnerable people on line whether they'd ever seen the real face of those who appealed to them on social media to leave all they knew. He quoted Islamic verses back to them in a context that showed love, not a justification for hatred. These men of peace now spread truth online, in their mosques, and especially in their homes. These people have success in changing those who might leave, and correcting those who want to come back. Young, aware, active Western youth from Muslim communities know their counter-arguments are the worst threat to extremists. These young Muslims know the recruiters for what they really are, liars. After all, is not one title of the devil the Father of Lies?

Intelligence officers always distinguished their jobs from the police with two expressions. The police wanted to 'nail 'em and jail 'em.' Intelligence officers said, 'Why burn 'em when you can turn 'em?' In short, a guy in a black hat could become a guy in a white hat someday. There are many, many jihadis who, like George Orwell before them, come to see the battle for what it truly is. Whereas the false god Orwell pursued was perfect equality 'just around the corner,' after class warfare, modern extremist Jihadism posits pure Islam after religious cleansing wars. Both wars were in reality only driven, relentless pain. Men in pursuit of power used in one case, equality, and in another, God, to recruit true believers. Today's young people will discover God was exploited as a recruiter's false pretext, used only to get them over there. Further, cynical manipulations, appeals to their manhood, their courage, and their need to feel wanted, keep them there.

If they want to come home, and there is evidence that is happening, there should always be an open door. Why is this? To feel trapped in a bad decision makes a man act from desperation. He'll fight on if he believes there is no hope of return. Cynical manipulators in ISIS keep this before their eyes, "There is no way out for you. You must now fight on, because you can't ever go back." ISIS cuts off their communication with the outside world; the jihadi hears only their point of view, because they want to control what he knows. Why else cut off the heads of Western journalists?

Instead, a disaffected jihadi must know there is a way home from the false god he has pursued. Our society, which must protect itself, holds the key to the door the changed jihadi must pass through. We need to be sure he knows it is available to him. Former recruiters and those of the Muslim faith who believe that modern men must live together in peace, tolerance, and dialogue can successfully bring these young people back. They can also protect them before such a radical departure is ever contemplated. Someday these Muslims too will produce an Orwell. One of them will perhaps write so as to bring down the facade of today's false god of radical religious extremism. Nothing will remain of it but a memory in a book. We need to support this.

A Salute to the Soldier Sent to Fight

What do the joggers on Washington's Mall
know of the men at the front?

They talk of a crisis in abstract
while the killing is left to the grunt.

Those who were never a soldier,
can always send others to die.

And all the fine reasons for warfare,
when spoken by them seems a lie.

So here's to the soldiers in combat,
but not to the talkers behind;

While the craven decided to spend you
I can't get you out of my mind.

VISITOR AND REFUGEE

He'd come to America from his Turkish homeland to visit his American relative's family. When we first met I was struck by his scholarly, quiet demeanor. It matched his career; he was a high school teacher. In the new calculus of his country, however, this was sufficient to make him an enemy of the state. He received notice while on vacation in America that his license to teach school in Turkey was revoked.

Indeed, his extended family might have been the cause of this revocation. They were not of the government's party. Of course, since his country now was in thrall to a dictator, he didn't know why he was deprived of his livelihood, and thus could not contest the decision. After all, to contest a government decree implies an appeal to the rule of law. But law was whatever the government whimsically decided it should be. Such an appeal could itself be proof of treason.

Thus the teacher joined the burgeoning ranks of the dispossessed. Since he was abroad, to return home meant incarceration and perhaps torture, as it did for many others already. He was forced to appeal to foreigners for refuge, in a land where he did not even speak the language. He was cut off from his livelihood, his family, and was a man without a country.

The Turkish coup took only those abroad by surprise. The Turkish government responded swiftly and surely to the poorly planned, almost ineptly executed attempt to overthrow the president. Bullets enough flew, but were shortly suppressed. No significant government buildings were taken, no media controlled. In fact even the bridges of Istanbul were held by soldiers unwitting of why they were called out. Some 300 people were said to have been killed.

Few believed this coup attempt was genuine. Many blamed 'outsiders', while the government blamed a man in America. Fethullah Gülen is a man in exile; he too is a man without a country. He is an Imam, that is, a Muslim cleric. He lives as a refugee in Pennsylvania. His Muslim followers believe in dialogue, interfaith tolerance, peaceful modernism, a free press, and open, ethical democracy. Indeed, he has said, "Tolerance, a term which we sometimes use in place of the words respect, mercy, generosity, or forbearance, is the most essential element of moral systems; it is a very important source of spiritual discipline and a celestial virtue of perfected people." Guelen is considered a dangerous person by the Turkish government.

His followers are many in both Turkey and elsewhere, having created an international school system in various countries. Emphasis is on science and technology, civics and foreign languages. They published what at one time was the largest, most progressive, peer reviewed and open newspaper in the nation of Turkey. They ran a television station, schools and universities, and sponsored international public conferences on education and religious tolerance.

For this, they were seen as a threat by the Turkish government, because in addition to learning, the followers of the teachings of Fethullah Gülen emphasized ethics, the rule of law and justice. They entered government, the military, academia, the press, and opened businesses and schools. Their aim was to practice goodwill toward all, religious tolerance, and to develop a technologically modern and free liberal democratic society. In doing so they exposed Turkish government corruption, nepotism, and international illegal sales of arms. Gülen's followers upheld the law, while the government wanted to hide its crimes, employ nepotism, and practice kleptocracy. For exposing this, Guelen supporters who were newspaper publishers, reporters, judges, military, and police officials were arrested.

When that did not stop the Guelenist pursuit of truth, the coup was opportunistically exploited by the government as a springboard to launch further arrests of thousands more Gülen adherents and even their family members. Yes, the tactic of arresting entire families, a Stalinist and Nazi- style practice outlawed even in medieval times, was employed. And not just military and civil service senior officers were targeted. Teachers were delivered cancellation of their certificates, police were fired, government officials and newsmen let go when their offices were taken over by the President's men. Simple people were oppressed as well, the better to drive away anyone who would question the government. In short, just as Field Marshall Goering used the burning of the German *Reichstag* to cancel democracy in Germany 'due to the emergency', so the Turkish government arrested thousands and incarcerated them, revoked their licenses, closed their newspapers, stole their businesses, and cancelled their military commissions because of the 'coup'. The newest Turkish building projects call for more…prisons. Those abroad at the time of this crackdown are now men without a country. This is how a dictatorship works.

Fethullah Gülen said, "Those who want to reform the world must first reform themselves. If they want to lead others to a better world, they must purify their inner worlds of hatred, rancor, and jealousy, and adorn their outer worlds with virtue."

This is the man the current government of Turkey calls a terrorist. The official name of the Guelenist movement is *Hizmet*, that is, Service.

A Side Trip to Hell

I digressed for a couple of hours on the road from Huntsville, Alabama to visit Andersonville, Georgia. This is the memorial site of a notorious Civil War prison where 13,000 Union soldiers died of starvation, disease, abuse, and neglect. Yet there is a little-known part of that story few know, a fact almost overlooked at the scene of this war crime.

Some years ago millions of Americans watched the powerful movie "Andersonville." In one memorable scene, six prisoners, condemned by their fellow inmates as murderers, are led to the gallows. The priest who accompanies them is not identified, and never speaks. This was a great oversight.

The Rev. Peter Whelan was an aged and bent 60-year-old Jesuit priest, quietly serving his diocese in Savannah, Georgia, when his pastoral ministry took a dramatic turn. With the coming of the war, he ministered to the Confederate soldiers stationed at Fort Pulaski in the nearby harbor.

In April 1862, the cannons of a Union fleet began a 30-hour bombardment of Fort Pulaski. Whelan was there, under intense fire, offering himself as a visible sign of God's presence to the many wounded and dying. With his fellow Southerners he, too, was taken as prisoner of war to Governor's Island, New York.

The enlisted men were shut up in a fortress called Castle William, a place of brutality and cold. It was cramped and pestilential. There was little food. Whelan became like a man possessed, demanding food, blankets, and clothing for his fellow prisoners. He wrote for material assistance to northern governors, military administrators and religious figures.

His efforts were by and large successful, until the arrival in June of Pulaski's wounded. Promised immediate release upon the surrender of Fort Pulaski, they were instead sent north to prison as soon as they could be moved.

Whelan's people were next sent to Fort Delaware, to a malarial island in that state. In the soldiers' vocabulary, however, it was soon renamed "Starvation Island." The argumentative whirlwind Whelan was offered immediate parole from the hell of prison if only he would go away. He refused. The shepherd remained with his flock until they were all exchanged in July 1862.

Back in Savannah, Whelan could not rest. He became aware of other prisoners, this time Union soldiers, to whom he could minister. These were held at a large Confederate prison near Andersonville, in his home state of Georgia.

The horrors of Andersonville are now well known. Unknown, however, are Whelan's heroic efforts. One soldier said, "… By coming here he exposed himself to great danger of infection… kneeling down by the side of decaying bodies… in the stench and filth of the gangrene wards… many and many a time I have seen him thus praying… His services were sought by all, for, in his kind and sympathizing looks, his meek but earnest appearance, the despairing prisoners read that all humanity had not forsaken mankind." Another observed, "Without a doubt he was the means of saving hundreds of lives."

When the prisoners had no food, Whelan took out a personal loan, and bought it himself. It became known as "Father Whelan's bread." He fed those who could not feed themselves. It was he who walked with the six condemned on the way to the gallows, seeking their reconciliation to God. He gave the thirsty drink. He clothed the naked. He buried the dead. Wherever the least outcast was to be found, so too, was Whelan.

He said of this time, "No amount of salary could induce me to stay at Andersonville for one week… not all the gold… in the treasury… It was to allay misery, and gain souls to God."

At war's end, he even spoke on behalf of Captain Wirz, the commandant of Andersonville, condemned as a war criminal. He believed Wirz was used as a scapegoat for all prison evils.

Whelan's legacy is not honored in a movie. It is best honored by a soldier whose life he saved at Andersonville, "...all creeds, colors, and nationalities were alike to him... He was indeed the good Samaritan."

Whelan never recovered his health. He died in 1869.

I thought about this story for quite some time. Father Peter had made his fundamental choice in favor of the belief there is neither Gentile nor Jew, slave nor free, Confederate nor Union. He concluded something simple. Each human deserved the dignity that comes with being made in the image and likeness of God. Man has no right to starve, freeze, beat or kill God. Father Peter's belief in these simple concepts led him to action. He became a living sign of Jesus' love, even in the hells of the American military prisons.

If you visit Andersonville today, south of Atlanta off I-75, you won't forget the visit. In addition to the actual site, there is now the National Prisoners of War Museum and National Cemetery. Due to the efforts of one man, Dorance Atwater, who secretly kept a copy of the burial records, and Clara Barton, who helped him publish them, all but 406 names of the Andersonville dead are known, and markers provided.

Oh, and one more remarkable site is there. It is called Providence Spring. Most of the deaths of the 45,000 men packed into Andersonville were due to disease caused by creek water that was used for all purposes. One day, during a terrible rainstorm which burst over the exposed prisoners, for they had no shelters but blankets, holes in the ground, and sticks, a lightning bolt struck the earth. Out gushed a freshwater spring beyond the 'dead line', where no one could go without being shot dead. The water flowed into the prison yard, and was fixed with a gutter, allowing men to drink, and live. You can visit this remarkable spring, too, which runs to this very day.

I reflected also that Father Peter was 60 years old when he began his prison ministry journey. In an era when few reached such an age, he literally became as a fiery prophet of old, for his was a titanic battle on behalf of the wretched, oppressed, and forgotten. His life shows that our time is not God's time. We can be called when we least expect it. All we have to do is watch, listen and pray. Then, when our time comes, we'll know it.

Terrorist Recruiters

There is much discussion today about how to 'prevent terrorism'. More specifically, thousands of analysts, and millions of research dollars, are poured into this study. What if the answer lies in front of us, unremarked, because unremarkable?

Imagine if I began by saying an American case officer recruited a source of information in the Soviet Union. Few would object, because this is a way we defended our country during the Cold War. Imagine now if I observed that a Nazi once pretended to be a democratic German, claiming to be part of a plot to overthrow Hitler. This false flag operative recruited a contact in British intelligence, whom he wanted to manipulate. Now we object, because we cannot accept the Nazi cause. What if a mysterious writer on the Internet enticed a young man to come to a war zone, and the youth went because he believed the disembodied writer represented all that was good about his faith? When next heard from, the young man had blown himself up in what he believed to be an act of martyrdom. Now we are in the realm of "radicalization", of "extremism", indeed of "terrorism" in today's lexicon.

Now imagine all the titles in the above examples, American, Soviet, Nazi, or terrorist suicide bomber, removed. We now have actions we can examine dispassionately. This is a way to study a problem if we want to understand.

In each of the cases I refer to, the recruiter is the actor who has a goal. The recruited is the person acted upon, because he has a weakness; not a motive, a weakness. Motive is very easy to determine. In most cases, as the old counterintelligence briefing had it, there was some sort of desire for money, ideology, compromise, or ego that could explain why a person did something. Yet wouldn't many of us agree we have similar sorts of motives in our own daily lives?

The recruiter is looking for a weakness. He wants to exploit the source's belief about something, to his, the recruiter's, advantage. A stevedore on the San Francisco docks in the 1940's, Eric Hoffer, wrote a book which came down to us today as the best, most explicit study on why men join mass movements. The True Believer spoke not of grand sociological issues, but rather of a single human's needs. A man who believed he had fallen from grace, be it through having his job taken from him, his family rendered hungry, his status disturbingly broken or unsettled, or his social standing demeaned, might feel compelled to join any movement, Communist, Nazi, supremacist, or other that offered a job, a hope, a vision, or indeed a faith. Hoffer spoke of his own post-Depression era of the 1940s, characterized by unemployment, despair, and fear about tomorrow. In short, among other like-minded people, the true believer found a renewed sense of belonging, indeed a vision for a better tomorrow. He felt a part of a community that looked forward to a golden age of virtue. It was said of 1930's Communists in Depression America "they had a kind of strength which perhaps no other group in America, conservative or radical, possessed." They offered, in the words of the former Communist Whittaker Chambers, "what nothing else in the dying world had the power to offer at the same intensity.... (a) faith and a vision." Arthur Schlesinger noted that the Chairman of the American House of Representatives, Hamilton Fish, observed "they are people who are willing to die for a religion."

Oddly, we Americans, in our misguided faith in secularism, stop here. We believe we should never consider religion, or more properly faith, in our calculus about terrorism. We must not discuss religion in the public square, because we consider it to be a private matter. And so it is, until it becomes public, despite what we profess to believe about it. How does the belief of another matter to me? Consider the young man who recently arrives in a new school. He feels himself an outsider, because he is. He doesn't belong, and is picked on by others. Lonely, and in self-defense, he finds others who will stick up for him. They might be a gang. To join them, to be accepted, or respected, he accepts what they do, and will do what they want. They are like the family to him that he doesn't have at his new school, or perhaps at all. Or, he seeks recognition in another way, by himself. He finds a gun.

Or, the lonely man goes another place where he is accepted, online. There he can be what he wants to be. He can be another person, indeed another race, class, or a totally different character. Or go back to what he thinks are his roots.

Yet he is still lonely. Perhaps he has given up his original faith, or quit practicing. He feels uneasy, having walked away from the faith he grew up in, or the family he had, or the society he lived in. Here online however, he finds that there are places where it is not only good to practice his faith, but respected. Here he learns that his problems of alienation are not because of anything he did, but because the social decay, the random hatred, and the lack of belief he sees around himself. All the world's problems are created by insufferable, heartless enemies, lost to God himself. He learns from his contacts on line, or in prison, or on the street, that others have found a way out of this corruption. He joins a faith. But what if that faith is represented by a Mephistopheles? What if the man who proposes the love of a vengeful God, or the workers' state, or the white race, or any other false god, is just another exploiter? What if he is just like the gang chief who said he cared for the lonely searcher, who took care of him, who got him respect, until he asked him to shoot someone?

A teacher in America wrote recently that she had a project which she practiced with every class she had, every week. She had them write down the kids they wanted to sit by, or who was a 'good citizen' that week. She was able, with these privately-submitted notes, to find out who always was mentioned, and who wasn't. She said she wasn't trying to set up a seating chart, or determine who was 'best citizen.' She was looking for the lonely, the outsiders. Then she took action to correct it, to reach out to them. She began this weekly practice after the massacre at Columbine. She practiced, to put not too fine a touch on it, real counterterrorism.

A London police officer once told me he would stop his patrol car, and spend time kicking a soccer ball with young people on a field in his district. Sharing time with them, he became someone they trusted, 'one of them', someone they could turn to. He was no longer a distant figure in a car, but a soccer playing buddy. And when there was trouble brewing, he'd be sure to hear about it.

A lonely, angry young man wrote a short story about shooting people crossing a street from an apartment window. Someone noticed, reached out to him, and changed his life away from a possible horrific end.

If we think we will defeat terrorism by a magic formula derived from a calculus of technology, we will fail. We can, however, stop the gang member, the shooter, or the terrorist before he becomes one. We must know ourselves, and then reach out to those who are lonely, or outsiders, or outcast. We do this in any way we can, wherever we find ourselves. Be it in school, or where we meet, or where we live, we can do it ourselves. Perhaps we can see it as part of our job to reach out and put professionals in touch with them, if necessary. We can do this anywhere, under any circumstances.

This is a new take on "If you see something, say something." Say something, or do something. But say or do it in a way that matters, in a way where action is taken. Take a bold new step even where it has never been done before, like that soccer game in London, or the quiet notes of a teacher, or a kindly approach to a lonely writer.

We can change the world. If we don't, there are certainly others who want to change it. They are recruiters, and they have blood on their minds. Because you see, they, too, are true believers. We have a world to win, against a determined foe, one lonely heart at a time.

As a spy catcher, I always wondered about those who recruited and then betrayed Americans they got to spy for them. The recruited spy wound up in jail, the spy recruiter escaped beyond the Iron Curtain, left with only his thoughts. Perhaps he thought like this.

SPY'S NIGHT THOUGHTS

It's only on a weary night, when darkness closes out the light, that I reflect and know I got away with it.

I got away with cold betrayal, a downright cold betrayal, with no penalty, no heart, and no forgiveness.

It's best they said, to do it cold, do it now and do it bold because you just can't live your lies forever.

So I betrayed the one whose trust, no, whose love...I ask you, now it's done, if whether lies...or a cold break...is better?

I never saw her face again, our lives are better broken then, where tears are not a matter to confuse us.

So yes I got unscathed away, the sorrow wasn't mine that day but now it's come back when I least expect.

I wonder that I wasn't hurt, wasn't caught in some dark work of others who would gladly pay me back.

Still others wondered at my skill: convincing sources in my way, and leaving them betrayed, and that was all.

So easy then to do again, easier still to do once more, until the only fear I had was failure.

Failure to betray at will, a cold and hangman's sort of bill, which masks an empty man beneath the posture.

Yes I was 'good' at secret plans which drew me like a drowning man; but never could escape the realization,

That all that first betrayal showed was how I hurt another soul, and I was just a just a bad man for my nation.

Open-Source Information: The Wild Card of the Modern Battlefield

Imagine the horror of death by friendly fire. See the faces of a mother and father at the moment they are told their son or daughter was killed by American fire. Today, far more than bullets can cause this horrific scene. This is a new age, and there are new threats.

Information warfare is the latest theme to capture the imagination of the U.S. Army. The modern Army, the technological army with the narrow soldier base, depends on the rapid and accurate flow of information to fuel its highly technical killing power. To protect its classified information, this army can depend on traditional security elements. This new army, however, also generates a massive amount of unclassified material that is overlooked by traditional security measures. Could this material reveal the secrets the Army hopes to protect?

In the information revolution, "open-source" information is the wild card of the modern battlefield. It is a form of friendly fire. The Army must protect this vulnerability through operations security. Information - its access, use, analysis and control - is clearly military matter. Classified information is protected by an array of security measures that are well known and practiced. But what about the literally millions of bits of unclassified personnel, logistical, operational, and supply documents that the Objective Force is generating? What can this information reveal and who will watch over it? What will protect this information that spews out over unsecured faxes, E-mail messages, and telephone networks?

The General is skillful in attack whose opponent does not know what to defend, and he is skillful in defense whose opponent does not know what to attack.—Sun Tzu 400-321 B.C

In the furor over recent revelations of Chinese espionage, who has asked how much they gathered from totally legal, totally open sources? What country will risk a major espionage recruitment when the same materials could be collected from an uncontrolled, open military website? Was it not Mao Tse Tung himself who counseled that, "the commander applies all possible and necessary methods of reconnaissance, and ponders on the information gathered, eliminating the false and retaining the true, proceeding from one onto the other, from the outside to the inside...?"

Does this not suggest collecting the unclassified until one can interpolate the secret? The Army must face this modern problem. Can the flow of information necessary to conduct operations hurt the Service? What if the unclassified material is so voluminous, so comprehensive, that it reveals the essential secrets the Army is otherwise so careful to protect?

At the beginning of World War II some 300 British engineers died because they could not defuse the new electrical bombs dropped by the Germans over England. It took trial and error and the chance discovery of intact electrical bombs on a downed German aircraft before the technology was defeated. Eight years earlier, in 1932, the technology for such bombs had been entered into the public records of the British patent office, yet none of the engineers knew about this open source of information.

Three hundred men died while the answer they sought was gathering dust in an unlikely place. Those who built the bombs that killed these men had found the information first and laid claim to it legally and openly. Had they known this, it would have been easy to convince the British people of the value of open-source awareness.

A shop-worn story of yesteryear? Are hired workers on North Atlantic Treaty Organization (NATO) compounds in the Balkans pacing off mortar ranges, as did the Vietnamese before them? Was it not the Belgian resistance fighter who said that people who experience occupation know the adversary better than he knows himself?

An earlier example involves the Maxim gun. When asked in 1884 why Western nations had colonized almost the entire known world, the English writer Hilaire Belloc said that it was not because of their advanced civilization, greater universities, or cultural advances. No, he quipped, "Whatever happens, we have got the Maxim gun, and they have not!" Of course, the technology for this early machine-gun and other technological information was routinely shared and sold in open contracts between "civilized" countries. In World War I this exchange of information resulted in the slaughter of an entire generation; by then all nations had access to the Maxim gun.

Military Intelligence

These stories show how open-source, openly available information works. What is routinely, even inadvertently given away today could kill someone tomorrow. Information that is not tracked could later surprise the Army on the battlefield. These stories about open-source information end in bloodshed. Is it inappropriate to say that the victims died from friendly fire?

Information is the lifeblood of the high-technology Objective Force. An array of information will deploy with the Objective Force wherever it goes, whoever the adversary is. Unlike most of the adversaries of the United States, whose technological developments are not shared openly, much of the information about our military's development is available to the entire world. For example, the Associated Press reported on a Pentagon armaments display showing soldiers with heat-sensitive night-vision sight, lightweight body armor, and computer backpacks. They reported concepts about laser warplanes, seagoing missiles, and more.

Today there are many armaments magazines, defense sites on the Internet, and newspapers reporting the business of warfare. These open-sources of information are cheap, readily accessible, and accurate. Through the eyes of a Western analyst, the publications are what they seem: military trade journals that cover market share, sales opportunities, competitive and joint ventures, and national acquisition goals. They are straightforward. Graphs and computer-generated art enhance the stories and illustrate the concepts. In the photographs used, sleek missiles fly, spotless armored vehicles roll, and wholesome, clean soldiers pose with the latest weaponry in pleasant pastures. There is no blood.

Consider now the reader of this same information from poorer, less industrialized, embargoed, or otherwise ostracized nations. Consider also the people of para-nations, ethnic clans, narcotics traffickers, and terrorists. They see the same information in terms of life-or-death choices. They cannot afford technical research or development, and they cannot "comparison shop." They know they must choose wisely the first time because there may not be a second choice. For them, the only collection method may be what they can learn from open publications. The more sophisticated groups can build on information from open sources and confirm their conclusions with traditional collection methods. Their interest is far from abstract.

Several truisms must be accepted in this new world of half-wars against non-traditional adversaries. Poorer nations want to survive. In order to do so they are offered the Hobson's choice of spending what wealth they have on arms or relying on a guardian nation to arm their people. They're not interested in future sales, in market share or in the bottom line. If they do not choose correctly from the arms necessary to protect themselves, they will cease to exist, or worse, be enslaved. Obviously, they see the world from a dramatically different perspective.

The West views military technology as a chess game. One player creates this; the opponent creates that to counter it, and so on. In this rational game of give and take, no one dies and the game goes on. Some call this the arms race, but nobody dies in a race. Such a sterile view of the industry misses the point.

Analysts of arms markets from non-Western countries or para-nations see the armaments industry differently and arguably more clearly than Western nations do. They, like the United States, will determine their needs and do all within their power and budget to acquire those necessities. Unlike the United States, they often see their existence as nasty, brutish, and short. They often feel they must confront the killer at the door, rather than the economic competitor in the pinstriped suit. It is not surprising that poorer countries decided to buy machine-guns as soon as they could afford them, once they saw what happened to those who did not. The callousness of the Western businessman who commented about a recent technology theft, "Who cares, we'll just build a counter-measure," would be incomprehensible to his counterparts in a poorer country who bet their very existence on successfully using proven technology in the near term. Those of poorer countries have a vested interest in what is available on the arms market today, and in knowing how their potential adversary will fight. What if their potential adversary is the United States?

These poorer countries want to know, simply put, how to beat the United States in battle. To be able to surprise the U.S. military, they will try to learn more about it than the military knows about itself. They do not have the wherewithal to conduct massive technical research, so they will take any shortcut. All open-sources will be exploited. Why spend the money on research and development if the final product is going to be for sale or is explained on the Internet? Why test weapons if the answers nations seek are printed in publications that cost only a few dollars each? Comparison tests will be done by those governments that see weaponry more as a commodity to be marketed than as a means of killing people.

Western powers think of long-term strategies while poorer nations wonder how to stop the immediate threat. They know they are dead if they make the wrong choices so they research information thoroughly. If they can piece together information about the true intentions of an adversary from what they can collect on the open-source market, they will do so. It may be the only source they have. These are the types of adversaries the U.S. military will confront tomorrow.

These differing perceptions of the world - one by rich nations, the other by poor - must be better understood. A poor man does not care about higher technology tomorrow if his weapon will surprise his enemy today. To achieve this he may act in a way contrary to what the West considers being in his best, rational interest.

Westerners must see the world with new eyes—their potential adversary's eyes. History offers many examples. In the 1920s, for instance, a beaten Germany, penned in by the Treaty of Versailles, entered joint ventures with Bofors Corp. of neutral Sweden. The Germans had studied the published armament policies of other European nations and had observed the soldiers occupying their country. They had studied what would win on a future battlefield, then set out to get it any way they could.

Before World War II, Germany illegally trained its army on the land of its arch-rival, the Soviet Union. Despite open reports of Germany's illicit training, other nations were too complacent to challenge this threat. The West was thinking about long-term, rational arms races. Germany was thinking about a *Blitzkrieg*. In a later example, the United States was shocked when it was revealed that the Vietnamese communists had routinely spliced into U.S. telephone lines. Open communications were compromised. These were simple farmers who should not have had the capability, the United States complained. The nation did not see the world through its adversary's eyes.

Today, are the Afghani or Iraqi government troops trained by us going to rest assured that the West will protect them? Did the Serbs or Muslims rely on the United States or NATO to take action against a vengeful adversary, or did they take their own measures? Does anyone doubt, however, that all soldiers and irregulars that deal with the U.S., be they on our side or against us, are devouring every statement and operational move we make in our many deployments? Every open document, every routine, every movement, every communication made by the U.S. military's soldiers is subject to collection or observation. Seemingly innocent communications could confirm or deny the fears of the many groups involved in Afghanistan or Iraq, not to mention Kosovo or Bosnia or Liberia. Seemingly innocent communications could confirm or deny the fears of the many groups involved in Afghanistan or Iraq, not to mention Kosovo or Bosnia or Liberia. How many American soldiers realize that a TDY order, supply form, repeated practice or logistical document could betray the military's true intentions?

Westerners may see no great loss when technology is compromised because they may never see the battlefield result of their work. They may think abstractly of their product as a funded program, not as something that kills someone. Their counterparts in another, less powerful country would face imprisonment or execution if they compromised hard-gathered information.

Westerners must "publish or perish." They have a "right to know," and a free and inquisitive press. Non-Western counterparts do not. The arms race fuels the West's ever-expanding market and the information-rich marketing ethic that advertises it. The military must create policies that protect all of its information—even the unclassified—because, in this new world, information that kills soldiers is a commodity available forsake.

Operations security, a process of securing this unclassified information, whatever its form, can protect the Objective Force. The security process is simple. Each element of the Army must ask itself, "What is it that I must protect, or else I'll fail in my mission?" The answer is that critical information must be protected, as Sun Tzu noted so long ago. Not everything that can compromise a mission is classified.

Next, the collection threat to this critical information must be studied. Soldiers must consider who wants what they have. Here, the intelligence community can provide assistance. The collection capability could be a highly sophisticated process or a hacker who can read the Army's E-mail. In weighing the threat to the critical information, the answer to the next question, "Is the Army vulnerable?" may be surprising. Even units with 100 percent traditional security of their classified information have been compromised by a hemorrhage of unclassified data. Unit leaders did not tell their soldiers what was critical to protect, and soldiers did not control bar talk, telephone talk, or what went out over the wire, much less what went into the trash. After the risks are weighed, such as collection capabilities and reaction times, countermeasures must be decided on. Even units with 100 percent traditional security of their classified information have been compromised by a hemorrhage of unclassified data. Unit leaders did not tell their soldiers what was critical to protect, and soldiers did not control bar talk, telephone talk, or what went out over the wire, much less what went into the trash. After the risks are weighed, such as collection capabilities and reaction times, countermeasures must be decided on.

The Army must communicate to accomplish any mission, but it has to remain aware of the unseen listener. Soldiers must know what an adversary can do. To survive, other countries will read everything the Army writes and listen to any conversation they can. The Army has to see itself as others see it. Once they learned that the Viet Cong had made tiny mines from discarded C-ration cans, soldiers stopped leaving cans uncontrolled. Now, the Army should do no less with its open-source information.

Czech Remembrance

We parked outside the Skoda Works in Plzeň, Czechoslovakia. The Iron Curtain had only come down a couple months before, and here we were outside one of the most famous industrial plants in central Europe. It supplied armaments to the Nazi war machine after the Czech nation was betrayed by the Western Allies at the Munich peace conference of 1938. The price of the 'piece of paper' which British Prime Minister Chamberlain agreed to with Adolf Hitler was almost seven years of occupation by German forces. Then came some 40 years of Communist police state dominance.

My family and I wandered down a side road, heading for the city square, with its mammoth cathedral. My sons, as usual, ran ahead scouting out the upcoming stores, unusual buildings, and cornices for strange carvings. We'd noticed they'd stopped in front of one window, which as we approached proved to be an antique store. They were enthralled by a wolf skin, prominently displayed for passers-by.

"Can we get it?" they asked, using the Royal we whenever there was some doubt as to the answer.

"Let's go in," I diplomatically replied. Inside, there was a huge array of strange items in a wondrous cabinet of curiosities. Items within came from of days long ago. They dated to when Czechoslovakia was part of a royal hegemony, then a democracy, then a dictatorship of the Brown Nazis, then of Red Communists. In these narrow rooms there was the history of a small nation sadly lodged between competing giants and ideologies. And then I noticed a picture, dated 1945, with a picture of American GI's in a tank, which liberated this part of the country after the Nazis were driven out. Unbeknownst to me, the owner had seen us looking at it. Then she must have overheard us speaking English to one another. She tentatively approached us and said, "You are Americans?" When we said yes, she said, "Wait."

Shortly thereafter, her daughter, some 13 years old, wearing a prim dress, with her hair in blond ringlets, appeared carrying a sheet of paper. Her hands trembled, as she held it before her, and read it as if a proclamation. "We welcome you, the first Americans to visit our store since 1945. We believe that you have a wonderful country, and we want you to know we love you." She might have said many, or a few, more things after that, but we were so overwhelmed with emotion that I couldn't hold back tears of simple joy. Simple joy. We hugged the little girl. We realized her mom might have been her age when the last Americans came through, only to leave again as part of our agreement with Stalin to trade huge parts of central Europe for half of Berlin. There were hugs and tears all around. We felt we could know, through their little letter, what it means to be free at last. This visit to an obscure little store, on a side street of an unremarked city of Europe, made all my time in Europe, fighting the Cold War, worthwhile.

EARTH

Our German friend from Leipzig, a retired engineer who'd once served in the former East German artillery, said he'd been under surveillance by the Communist government since he was 17. Even in the former Communist German Democratic Republic, where he'd lived, that was hard to believe. He was 62 when he told this story. The Berlin Wall and Iron Curtain had been down only a couple years.

"I went on a field trip to the Soviet Union with my senior high school class. It was to be a typical show of German-Soviet Socialist Brotherhood. They would take us to Moscow, and show us the battlefields where the Nazi Fascists had been defeated by the Red Army. Before I went, my aunt asked me a favor. 'Could you please bring me back a spoonful of earth from where your uncle died near Moscow when you visit there?' This was fine with me.

"As we got into Moscow, I left our dormitory one late afternoon and set off to find a war cemetery. I couldn't read Cyrillic, but wandered until I found the subway system. From there I asked, using hands and feet, where a war cemetery was, or any cemetery. Directed there, I went up to ground level, and walked until I found a cemetery. Then, using a spoon in my compound knife, I took up some earth, and put it in a bag. After more adventures, I found my way back to the group. No one had missed me during the free time. I only noticed that my notebook, with all my friends' names, was missing. I thought I'd mislaid it somewhere, and didn't worry about it.

"I was only arrested once during the DDR (Deutsche Demokratische Republik: East Germany) time. My friend and I wanted to hear jazz, but our city of Leipzig was very old-fashioned. So we drove to Czechoslovakia. On our return we were arrested at the border, and interrogated for many hours, since the idea of jazz was heretical under the communist system. They finally let us go home.

"Yet let me tell you of a strange story, which I myself cannot believe. With the fall of the Wall, many of the less important Stasi (secret East German police) files were captured by the freedom movement. With the reunification of Germany, you can now request your own files kept on you by the DDR Secret Police. So I did. What I found in those files shocked me. I want to tell you that story.

"On a certain day, our doorbell rang. We lived in an apartment complex, so the person who rang it had to ring all of the bells until he reached me, whom he didn't know. Now, I was known to be very good at repairing Trabis. (Trabant cars, 2 cylinder cars manufactured in the DDR). He asked if I was the man in the building who was good with cars, since his had broken broke down outside. He said he'd asked a passer-by for help, who told him I was good with cars. I gladly went out and repaired the minor problem. So began our wonderful friendship, which lasted almost twenty years. He and his wife became our friends, and we met each other often for family occasions, or just to enjoy one another's company.

"When I read the files, I became heartbroken. I discovered that my trip as a high school boy to the cemetery had been carefully surveilled. In fact, when they saw what I did, they secretly assigned me a code name, *Erde* (which means earth), for the spoonful I brought back to my aunt. This is the code name they used whenever they wrote about me during the rest of the history of the DDR! Then I saw a black notebook fall out of the file. They had taken my notebook in Moscow when they finished the surveillance. I'm sure all my friends became possible suspects from that day forward. My friend and I were also noted as possible threats to the homeland because we enjoyed jazz, considered a bourgeois deviation in straight-laced DDR times. And then I read the story of the broken-down car. The entire story of the broken-down car was a calculated, orchestrated deception. They wanted to get someone in constant contact with me through a natural setting, and created this incident. Imagine, my friend of twenty years was writing reports on me whenever they needed one. His friendship was all a sham. Can you imagine, all those years, all those man hours! What was the Stasi secret police other than a criminal gang of make-work policemen? Why were they so afraid of us?"

PART IV: LANGUAGE ARTS

If you make listening and observation your occupation, you will gain much more than you can by talk.--Robert Baden-Powell

OUR ACHILLES' HEEL: LANGUAGE SKILLS

Imagine you are a soldier in Iraq or Afghanistan. Wouldn't you feel safer if your combat leader was a linguist and conversant with local customs? What if your company's intelligence was provided by an illiterate? What if your best translator was someone the locals despised or considered to be a spy?

How can we distinguish between the respected, the thugs, the honest, or the dregs of a foreign society, if we cannot understand what they say to us? We Americans have a cultural bias against learning languages other than English, but now our soldiers' lives depend on our doing so.

How accurately and well we analyze the indigenous people we deal with during the Global War on Terrorism might well determine the success or failure of counterinsurgency operations. Our combat training will be for nothing if our linguist does not tell us the truth or fails to recognize it because of a lack of training. A lack of foreign language skills is our Army's Achilles' heel. Timeliness and accuracy are everything in intelligence, and thus, a linguist's skills are more important than firepower. With the former, you might not need the latter.

Foreign language skills are mission-essential for an expeditionary army. Our soldiers die in foreign lands because American comrades they can absolutely trust lack those skills. We forget that our job is to move, shoot, and communicate, and we forget that "communicate" does not refer just to radios.

When we conduct a raid and find no one there, what was the cause? Was the intelligence bad? Did we give the mission away because of poor operations security? Were we led to the wrong target? Were we too late in getting there? Was the enemy tipped off that we were coming? Is it possible our linguist missed a critical nuance because of his lack of skill? Where should the damage assessment begin? Who knew the truth? And who translated it for him?

For Want of a Language

Pham Xuan An, who wrote for *Time Magazine*, was a secret Communist spy during the Vietnam War. Erudite, witty, and insightful, he was said to be a pleasure to deal with. Ideologically motivated, he worked to destroy us. At the other extreme is the Iraqi who makes a separate peace because if he does not the enemy will kill his family. Both types of spies (for the lack of a better word) gain access to our plans because of their skill in the English language and our ignorance of theirs. The way into the American fortress is through the open gate of language. No traitor betrays us; our lack of training does.

Platoon leaders and operations center chiefs rely on linguists. Linguists are the interpreters on the streets for our patrols and the translators of recently recovered documents. For better or worse, we rely on who is available when we deploy. Army officials predicted a need for hundreds of Arabic speakers before Operation Iraqi Freedom. The Army ended up with forty-two. We deployed 140,000 troops to Iraq with 42 interpreters!

A Perishable Skill

Unless a soldier has learned Arabic as a child, or any other language for that matter, he will find conversing in it a perishable skill. Few retain a language without frequent practice with those who can conduct serious, adult conversations. Of the forty-two linguists deployed during Operation Iraqi Freedom, probably only half could speak the language intelligently.

The ability to speak a foreign language skillfully cannot be put in cold storage in the hope that it will sparkle again someday. Communicating with words is one level of skill, but to understand nuance, culture, and traditions is another. The latter should be a career pursuit. The Army, however, does not offer its soldiers such an opportunity. As a fighting force, we are utterly dependent on linguists for field intelligence, to help in rapport building, and for the many unexpected missions that befall occupation soldiers. Linguists speak with information sources, interpret important documents, and even read road signs for us.

Desperately Seeking Interpreters

All the financial assistance we allocate, and all the infrastructure and civic affairs we provide must be explained to Iraqis and foreign nationals by someone. The more reliable that person is the better. The usual Army method is to seek out foreigners who speak the English language, but this often means tapping exclusively into Westernized groups. In Vietnam, we relied on French-Vietnamese Christian elites who had little, if any, contact with the country's Buddhist population. In Bosnia, we dealt with anyone who spoke English, regardless of his background, about which we usually knew next to nothing. Our Somali translators were ex-taxicab drivers granted interim security clearances.

Nothing has changed in Iraq; our understanding of local social hierarchies is limited at best, a matter of total ignorance at worst. There are people you do not deal with in some societies and others who are invaluable when you are attempting to understand an entire culture, not just its parts. When problems arise regarding local customs, traditions, taboos, and social mores, someone who has spent his professional career understanding such issues is a god-send. (Of course, without such a person, you do not realize you have the problem in the first place.) Absent a culturally astute American linguist, we are forced to rely on whoever can help us muddle through. Ours, the most thoroughly trained, best-equipped Army in history, relies on virtually unknown foreigners vulnerable to insurgent death threats. How long will they valiantly resist threats to their loved ones before they betray us?

Training Our Own

How can we train our own effective translators? Those who study languages must understand the long-term utility of devoting themselves to years of rigorous study and practice. Unfortunately, there is no career path for officers to pursue this skill, and money incentives alone cannot do it. In the 19th century, the British Foreign Office assigned a man to a country more or less for his entire career. He became the man on the spot, the go-to civil servant who could be relied on to know his area and the personalities resident there. But there will never be a Lawrence of Arabia in the U.S. Army. He would be reassigned seven times or more before he developed the expertise Lawrence had.

Foreign-language training must involve constant immersion. As a graduate of the Defense Language Institute (DLI), I would implement immediately a Berlitz-like foreign-language-only teaching regimen there. Assignments for graduates in their target countries should be either at embassies or consulates if no military bases require their presence. Assignments that demand interacting with local nationals should be highly sought after and rewarded as much as any other service position. No graduate of DLI should be allowed to live on-post. His job is to interact with the locals. How better to do so than to live among them? When I was assigned to Germany, I knew three words for light machine-gun, but not one for diaper. It was through common, everyday dealings with young German families that I learned their words and ways and became better at my liaison job. Foreign area officers should also be assigned to foreign units. They should attend foreign schools; in fact, it should be a job requirement to do so.

Employ Incentives

We have native-born Americans who study languages at some of the finest universities in our land, yet we offer them nothing in the way of incentives to employ their language skills in an Army career. We have citizens who speak every language in the world. They are first- or second-generation immigrants. Yet the Army has not tapped into that linguistic reserve programmatically by encouraging them to help us become truly combat effective in the lands of their ancestors.

The Army must offer a career path for linguists. A good speaker of a foreign language is an asset. A trusted, trained language professional can save many lives. It is time to do something about the Army's Achilles' heel.

THE LANGUAGE PARADOX

I let my M-1 Garand do my talking!--WW II Poster, showing battle-scarred soldier

All men dream: but not equally. Those who dream by night in the dusty recesses of their minds wake in the day to find that it was vanity: but the dreamers of the day are dangerous men, for they may act out their dream with open eyes, to make it possible.-- Lawrence of Arabia, **Seven Pillars of Wisdom**

In Iraq, a Marine sniper team was placed on a top floor in a bandit heavy neighborhood. Suddenly, all action stopped. For two days there was no action at all. Then the mystery was solved. A Marine saw something taped on the door leading into the team's building. On a piece of masking tape, written in magic marker, a message in Arabic read, "Attention! There's an ambush with American snipers inside the building!" For six days, no one paid attention to the unreadable sign on the door. The team was resupplied, changed over, and waited for enemy activity that never happened. No one could read the sign which warned the enemy away.

This story is legion throughout American war efforts. We don't have the linguists, and we need to ask ourselves why. America, more than any other country, draws its people from every land on earth. Yet, we are considered all around the world as a people of only one language. In counterinsurgency war, this costs lives.

America is a melting pot. Generations ago, immigrants considered learning English as a mark of having become Americans. Indeed, it was considered a mark of backwardness to still speak the language of the 'old country.' This is an attitude we often carry into combat. It is a mistake to do so.

Military people like action. We are impatient with inaction, not to mention a lack of apparent, quick results. Notice that the goal of a combat soldier is to 'move, shoot, and communicate'. Moving and shooting are clear enough, and communication for the combat veteran usually deals with his radios. But insurgency warfare is a different story altogether. The ability to communicate refers more to literally linguistic communication. It means communicating in a foreign language. We as Americans have, as we have seen, a cultural bias against the multi-linguist. Even in the intelligence fields, we do not properly understand his many roles.

In the military services, we generally think of the linguist, if at all, as a sort of local who is a mission add-on. He is the translator who is called on to talk to 'the indigs'. Little if anything is known of him. We don't know his family connections, his ethnicity, his history. Nor do we know his interests, his prejudices, his dreams for the future. In fact, that someone can speak English seems to make him 'one of us.' This results in a paradox. We seem to think the foreign English speaker is acceptable, although in a lowly capacity where we really don't trust him. Too often, we ignore him, as if he weren't there, or had no thoughts or dreams himself.

The State Department, however, has identified many missions for the linguist which the services would do well to note in this era of counterinsurgency warfare. They are translators and interpreters, but also information collectors, reporters, documentation managers and reviewers. They conduct research and serve in advisory capacities; they teamwork with planners at every level. Have the services thought through their own use of linguists to this extent? How do the services plan to 'communicate' their objectives to their local counterparts?

We seldom, if ever, realize that proper use of a linguistic capability would not only advise about local cultural imperatives, local grievances, and practices, but even preclude many unnecessary military actions. For instance, a young Staff Sergeant, who taught himself some Arabic, was advised by Iraqi police 'not to go down this road' on a certain day. It turned out that the road had been mined the night before. Leave aside how these police knew of the actions of the enemy, and took no action. They wanted to keep their personal friend alive, their friend who could speak to them.

One friend of mine, a former Army officer with great insurgency experience, has said that the perfectly employed linguist can serve the role of the best policeman. He will know the streets, and the people. He'll be able to read the reality of the environment, and advise accordingly. My colleague even offered a methodology to confirm this linguist's abilities, through double checking with a trained American linguist. Linguists could be our best intelligence officers. Americans can learn, indeed grow up in many cases, with the target languages of the countries we are involved in. American linguists who are also intelligence officers could be involved in the most secret of planning. They can be relied upon where the foreigner, involved in direct pressure in his own country, cannot. We seem to forget that.

General "Vinegar Joe" Stilwell knew this intuitively. A Chinese linguist, he was the military attaché to the Chinese government of Chiang Kai-shek during their war against Japan in the 1930's. Stillwell sought out some five other Chinese-language trained American Army officers. He assigned them to five different regions with orders to send him unvarnished, on-sight truth from the battlefields. Armed with these actual reports from linguists present at the events, Stilwell was able to advise the US Government on further US military actions.

Today, there is no career field for a dedicated area linguist officer. Only the Foreign Area Officer comes close, and then only for a short period of time. There would never be a Lawrence of Arabia in the American Military.

There are, indeed, several initiatives to partly rectify this vast lack of reliable linguists. There is the first-ever Army language company, comprised of some 140 vetted, native speakers of the Arabic, Farsi, Pashtu and Kurdish languages so lacking in our Army. Interestingly, the previously mentioned paradox is also overcome, for combat leaders are more relaxed with soldier-linguists in uniform. The FBI is actively seeking linguists, and the CIA is chasing ever more linguistic capable recruits. There is even a massive effort to recruit among the immigrant populations of America, offering expedited citizenship to those who qualify.

There is, in the end, nothing we cannot do. First, we must overcome the cultural bias against the linguist, and see that he holds a valuable position, a position which can be employed at every level of military service. Secondly, we must make it a career path, for enlisted and officers alike. Thirdly, we must understand that there are many, many venues where this skill can manifest itself, as the State Department has long known. In the end, it will reward us by saving lives. When we properly employ linguists, we won't have to 'let our M-1 Garand do our talking.'

THE TRUSTED TONGUE

After a presentation on Force Protection, I met the speaker privately as he prepared to leave. "During all that year in Iraq, did you ever completely trust your foreign translator?" I asked.

The general was momentarily taken aback. He became reflective. He said, "No one ever asked me that question." Then, deliberately, he responded "No. No, I never did."

This candid response speaks volumes about a boil in our collective military boot. We fail, almost every time, when we go into counterinsurgency roles. We do not have, and do not have a means of producing, sufficient trained, cleared, and reliable linguists.

Americans, however, have stumbled onto ingenious uses of linguists. Recall the Code Talkers, the Navajo Indians who defeated Japanese radio interceptors. Consider too Japanese-American Nisei communicators on the Italian peninsula in World War II, outwitting German radio monitors. The value of ready, American linguists is not unknown, simply unexploited. We value it, but not enough to plan for it.

Vast sums have been invested in trying to create and buy language technology, hire contractors, and train native-speaking service members once we are committed to a lengthy counterinsurgency. We've had mixed results, but mixed results aren't good enough when lives are at stake. We need one characteristic above all: trust. No technology, no cultural awareness course, no training creates a trusted linguist. We require more than a proliferation of mushroom like quick fixes.

Native linguists are subject to threats to their families still in the country. The fear of his mother's head on his doorstep, or his extended family disappearing, will undermine the most engaged linguist's enthusiasm. This is why we were always cautious of East-European Americans who had family behind the Iron Curtain. Their families could be compromised, and they in turn blackmailed. So where does that leave us?

We have the answer, and we've had it all along. As early as high school Junior ROTC we can encourage the study of languages. Imagine a student assembly where rewards are given to the budding linguist who gets an A in French, as well as the player selected for the football team. Imagine that award for language excellence presented by the Professor of Military Science. This has never happened, but it should. Such encouragement, at such an impressionable age, by someone respected for his uniform, could lead to great things for the student, indeed for our country.

So, too, in our universities. I recall no encouragement to study a foreign language when I was in college. If someone from the ROTC department had done so, and had shown me the military-related reasons for so doing, I would have jumped at the chance. Imagine a program specifically for language study sponsored by the government. Such a clear road map could be the answer to so many young people wandering the halls of academia. Certainly it would enrich the young linguist, and be a boon for our military and country later.

The objection might be that students would opt for a semester abroad in France rather than Oman. The size of college grants could be rated by the difficulty of the language, and grade point average. Chinese grants could trump German. A minimum grade point average would be the glue that holds the grant in place. Yet, is university language study alone the point?

Solutions begin with honesty. A young linguist, introduced to the value of language study by a mentor from the services, will make a good officer. Ideally he'll work in his field of study, growing in awareness and appreciation of the nuances of his mission area. Yet, if the mission requires other languages, he won't be afraid, or shocked, to accomplish that mission too. He'll know it can be done, what is required to do so, and that he can do it.

The Loyal Translator Dilemma

The Dutch boy was hoisted onto the Sherman Tank's skirt near the end of World War II. His beaming smile revealed his joy at being selected by the American liberators to guide and translate for them as they drove through winding Netherlands country roads.

He led them through twisting medieval streets, intervened with confused, exuberant, or questionable locals, and helped them win the day. He was a good linguist, a clever advisor, and thoughtful guide.

American soldiers engaged in combat in the Netherlands were not only cheerful friends of Dutch youth; there was a reason for their reticence to trust adults. The GIs had been warned to trust only children, because it was widely believed that Dutch resistance was thoroughly compromised by German counterintelligence. Any translators might be spies, or worse, saboteurs who would lead Allied soldiers into ambushes.

This story is echoed today. Our Army once again finds itself with a linguist dilemma. It comes down to this: Do you trust the man who is telling you what the locals say? What can the Army do to insure we can deploy numerous, capable, and loyal linguists in a future conflict?

Every war demands great linguistic skills. America can be justly proud of the Nisei Japanese radio operators. Their communications helped save lives and win battles, such as Iwo Jima, where Old Glory became the Marine Corps' icon. Cajun French linguists worked endlessly with French civilians and resistance fighters to guide Allied soldiers across Normandy after D-Day. Just like the Navajo linguists who quickly transmitted messages in a 'code', so too Jewish New Yorkers came to the rescue as Counter Intelligence Corps debriefers in war-torn Germany. All these linguists were devoted soldiers, and loyal Americans. I suggest they embodied a truism. Skilled, culturally attuned linguists are force multipliers, but loyal linguists are battle winners.

The question each war's linguist requirements brings with it comes down to loyalty. Do you trust this man or woman to translate this document properly, interpret that conversation correctly, advise on the proper cultural approach, convey the whole message, or guide the team? If the answer is "I'm not sure, such doubt hovers over every action our military must take. Situational awareness should not include doubting, or indeed fearing, your own translator.

Consider how translators have secretly conveyed messages to prisoners in Guantanamo. Others have falsely advised when translating battle field intelligence, sometimes by committing errors, or leaving out significant facts.

Secret enemies posing as translators have led convoys into ambushes. A translator even set himself afire on the very field our Secretary of Defense and senior Allied General traversed.

One particularly sinister event found locals telling an American not to go down a trail the following day, because they knew of an ambush. No one ever thought to ask how they knew.

On the other hand, some translators are truly noble, embodying every good feature of a comrade in arms. They are someone you might trust with your life, or risk your own life for. One American guerrilla fighter desperately attempted to save his source, left waiting on a dock, from the wrath of the oncoming North Vietnamese.

What if any is the difference between World War II and now? The requirements to field many translators are the same. So are the missions. Yet why can this country not find linguists who can carry the admittedly significant burden ready, available, and clearable? For, burden it is. Fully 40% of the casualties suffered by contractors in the early years of the Iraq war were linguists. They are often looked upon by the locals as collaborators, or worse, traitors. They do not look upon them as Nathan Hales, but Vidkun Quislings. What motivates a man to work for us, if work is how he sees it? Much depends on where he comes from, and that is where we must find the resolution to the loyal translator dilemma.

Translators are required for virtually every encounter of US forces with local people. Linguists are required in abundance for document exploitation, translation of telephone, radio, computer, and other interceptions, and any intelligence activity directed against a foreign element. We must have them, or cause potential actionable intelligence to be abandoned. Every senior officer seeks them to be their 'go-to guy' for local cultural communications, and often this is where they are most dangerous. The spies know we need them, because as one wryly observed, " Americans are masters of gathering intelligence, but they don't know what to do with it."

Pham Xuan An was just such a fixer. From his coffee table at Café Givran in Saigon, the diminutive but dapper Vietnamese stringer could interpret, analyze, and assist with any dilemma faced by newsmen, GIs, and later, senior officers and major news agencies. He was a truly remarkable confidant, for when not working wonders for the Americans in South Vietnam, his services to North Vietnam as a spy caused even Ho Chi Minh to exclaim with joy when his reports arrived, "We are now in the United States' War Room!"

Do you recall such a man, or woman? It matters not which war, but each war produced someone like this. We Americans are particularly vulnerable because we rely heavily on local hires to do our interactions with the native populace. We trust our vetting to assure their loyalty.

What can you reveal about yourself to your translator? How far can you believe in him, to the point that you can entrust knowledge which will directly, perhaps completely, affect the mission, and your very lives?

Traditionally linguists come from recruitment in the host country's zones of conflict. These are best qualified in localisms, cultural awareness, and area knowledge, but are least trustworthy. Or, they come from elsewhere, drawn from the world pool of nationalities and ethnicities. These too require constant vetting, checking, and testing. They come from recent American immigrants. These immigrants are known, cleared, but less trained in cultural awareness, language skills, and nuanced appreciation of the conflict area, their former native land. This complex concern has faced every American Army. How can we hope to resolve this dilemma today, knowing we will soon face the same Gordian knot in the next conflict?

America is a land of untapped linguistic skills. We can make America a model to the world in language and cultural development. Those skills, thoughtfully nurtured and developed, can become a national asset. They will make us more aware, sensitive, and competitive. Such can be a godsend for our Army's future deployments.

American schools are now being chartered where students study French, Arabic, Chinese, and other languages all day. These schools are being developed to accommodate kindergarten through high school. Also, experiments have shown that American children, with only one or two years of day-long study of a foreign language, emerge fully fluent. American students who have such skills can qualify for study abroad during advanced education, which not only broadens their horizon as people, but makes them truly national assets. They are available to interact for America with the country of their foreign language skill.

Consider how the Army can benefit from such charter programs. Funding targeted foreign language study at an early age, when language learning is easy, fun, and self-consciousness is not an issue, could be initiated through the Department of Defense. Some of the young people who attend such study could one day qualify for advanced study abroad, subsidized by Army funding, against a service obligation. The service obligation would be honored by employment in the country of interest, or in a mission directly related to that country's activities.

These Americans could be our own go-to people. They could be our young officers whose cultural awareness imitates the abilities of even that legendary Lawrence of Arabia. We must be more sensitive to the abilities a linguist deploys. One officer, a master of five Southeastern Asian languages, was drawn away from working against active insurgencies because he lacked a mandatory deployment, unrelated to the guerrilla missions he was fighting. This happened in order for him to attain 'career development'. If his career was not fighting wars for which he was uniquely qualified, then what else was? In the documentary drama about Violette Szabo, British Special Operations Executive agent, there is a symbolic scene where she appears wearing a striking dress at a British Officer's Club in London. Several women comment, "Doesn't she know there's a war on?" They did not know she had bought it on the black market in Paris where she had just been, coordinating resistance groups because she was bilingual.

Whose job is it to care about linguist employment as much as other career fields? Could it be because there is no career field for the linguist? Consider again how important this role is. It could be due to a linguist's liaison that an entire Army does not have to deploy. Remember, Lawrence of Arabia was not only a liaison officer, but mobilized the Hejaz uprising against the Turks in World War I. Our Special Forces know the value of such skills. Today they work hard at maintaining such skills as they once did among the Hmong people, and today in Afghanistan.

We can employ Americans' linguist skills as we would any vital national asset. We must be at least as good a steward of these perishable skills as we would be of a battle tank. A linguist, properly employed, is more valuable than a tank. Indeed, he is what might make it unnecessary to deploy that, or any other tank. What we need is a career field for the Non-Commissioned officer, Warrant, and Commissioned officer in a language discipline.

Employ young, cleared, and ready linguistic and culturally trained soldiers only where they are of service to the Army. They will be the

Special Forces soldier, the liaison officer, the Advisor of host nation armies, the staff advisor or translator of documents. Employ them, as our Special Forces do now, in targeted areas of the world, with good cultural training, language maintenance, and career paths, to achieve victory in the next conflict.

Ours is a heritage of the brave frontier fighter, but the battles of our future will seldom be the fair gunfight. Rather, they are often characterized by espionage, deception, ambush, and subtle ambiguity. The way out of the jungle is to shine a light, a light which a loyal linguist can provide, again and again. Loyal linguists are battle winners.

DISINFORMATION

I was prompted to write this essay when I read the book, Disinformation.
This sinister employment of lies and language must be made known to
those subject to its wiles and deceits.

Communist Romania wanted Lieutenant General Ion Pacepa dead. He defected to the West at the height of the Cold War, and carried with him a story which will change the way you will read history. He, together with legal professor Ronald Rychlak of the University of Mississippi, give us the background on 'disinformation'. This sinister word makes real what George Orwell described as Newspeak, for it distorts truth to convey lies. Pacepa and Rychlak show how disinformation is as much a part of Communism as Karl Marx.

Pacepa was the highest ranking former East Bloc spy chief ever to defect to the West. In 1978, after 23 years climbing the bitter mounds of deceit which Communism had become, he'd had enough. He would not assassinate for his country. He did, however, make known to the West how the Communist bloc lied to destroy reputations of those they feared.

Under guidance from the Soviet Union, innuendos and then accusations based on forgeries, false witness, blackmail, and perjury were employed to ruin the reputations of leading post-World War II clergy and leaders. The Red goal was to destroy people's respect for leaders of the various governments and churches in each of their subject countries. The Communists could thus eliminate formidable barriers to complete victory. Churchmen who had bitterly opposed the Nazis were "framed" into looking as if they had been Nazi stooges during the Hitler occupation. Thus cardinals, bishops, and priests were lied about. When they did not confess to false charges, to perjured witnesses, and forgeries, they were tortured to sign bogus confessions, forged with their 'own' handwriting by experts. Even Pope Pius XII, the great defender of Jews and others persecuted by Nazis, was attacked by communist innuendo through a play, The Deputy, and a host of other falsehoods calculated to cast lies as truth.

Pacepa goes on to trace how these techniques were employed throughout the Cold War to make Israel appear to be a Zionist co-conspirator with America with the aim of subverting the Middle East. He demonstrates how even in America the sinews of false leads, disguised motives, and 'leaked lies' were used by communist conspirators to weave a false narrative of our national goals.

Pacepa is at his best when he describes his time as the chief of Rumanian intelligence. He tells of receiving direct orders from Moscow. Together with Rychlak, he conclusively demonstrates the insidious plot behind the character assassination of religious leaders under Communism. Pacepa's speculations regarding events after his defection are rightly limited to showing how subversive actions against US policies could have been initiated by disinformation. He further demonstrates how disinformation campaigns, once they start, often take on a life of their own. Read the book, then re-read the history of the Cold War.

Language and Citizenship

Many hundreds of years ago, in the early days of America, a traveler would have faced a daunting linguistic challenge. The continent was massive. It included vast areas of mountain and desert, enormous grasslands, and dense green forests. Over 500 different native tribes populated the hills, valleys, and plains. Yet it was possible to travel, and be understood, even then. There was a common sign language, which was known to all, so that simple communication could take place.

As philologists we understand how important this is, for without communication there is no hope for dialogue, and without dialogue, there is no hope of understanding the world as the other person sees it. If we can't do that, we cannot begin to build bridges, which is the theme of this conference. Why do we want to do this? Without bridges we never know what that person on the other side of the river thinks, believes, or loves. We can never really understand them, or they us, and so we can never really work toward common goals together. A bridge doesn't make us the same, but it helps if we want to cross it.

So where do we begin? It is the same question we could ask if we said, why would anyone want to travel? Consider this: to truly have a dialogue with another person, it is important to know what is important to him. We have to know what certain important words mean to our foreign counterparts. No one wants cultural or linguistic imperialism, which is based on the false assumption that you think just like me and understand certain words just as I do. How can we reach a true understanding of someone else, while at the same time allowing that person to learn what is true about us? Only in such a way can we work toward mutual understanding, friendship, reconciliation, and the greatest goal of all, peace.

In the early 1990's, my wife taught an English as Second Language course. In the class was a young lady who had come to America from a former Communist country, to be an au pair for an American family.

But that job was only the means that brought her to America; it was not the reason why she really came. She came because she had seen an American movie, *Dances With Wolves*, and wanted to see for herself the vast, wonderful land she had seen on the screen. America was a land where endless prairies and giant buffalo herds still existed. She wanted to meet the people that lived in such a place, and get to know them and understand them. This is really why she came, because she had a dream of understanding America, and Americans.

As students of languages we know that progress only really starts once you have mastered the basics. First you have to understand verb forms, sentence structure, idiomatic expressions, and grammar. Yet once we have achieved that, where do we go? How can we truly understand the people whose native language basics we have just mastered? Do we ever find ourselves asking questions like that posed at the beginning of this presentation, "In that country do they mean justice just as we do?"

I suggest that a new form of language training can help here. It would cost nothing, but it would be a true gift to the new arrival, the student, the aspiring citizen, or simply the traveler who comes and hopes to learn something of the land and people she or he is visiting. How does this idea work? I maintain that we can teach what is fundamentally important to the people of any nation by teaching the language associated with that country's citizenship requirements. Let's consider the case of American English, but this idea could apply equally to any language, taught anywhere.

"...nothing so liberalizes a man and expands the kindly instincts that nature put in him as travel and contact with many kinds of people."- Samuel Clemens, (Mark Twain), Letter from San Francisco published June 23, 1867

If you hear the word English, you think of England. Yet we Americans speak English, the Irish speak English, even the Australians speak English. We are all quite different. I contend that for the traveler to understand a people, he must first discover what is important to them, why they are different.

Yet what exactly does that mean? And how do we discover this?

I propose that for someone to understand the American personality, he needs to understand why we are Americans, and not, well, someone else from some other country. How can we tell the difference? What is American instead of Canadian, or British, or West Indian? Just as our accents and our idioms distinguish us one from another, so too does our heritage. Now we are no longer talking about rote facts such as grammar, sentence structure, and spelling. We are talking about ideas. To learn these, it is important to advance in our study of the language of a given culture. It is at this level that my language proposal becomes significant.

When I lived in the Netherlands, one of the gifts that country offered a visitor was free language training. They understood that the easiest way to learn about a country was to learn its language. The goal was to provide the basis to begin communicating.

When I was learning German, my professor would invite me to lunch, open a German lexicon and tell me, "Point". I would point at some subject at random, and we would talk about that theme throughout lunch. The goal was to expand my vocabulary. I specifically recall talking about penguins, Ethiopia, killer whales, even tattoos. Of course, I must admit I had little opportunity to speak on these subjects in my later life, though I tried my best to bring them up at every occasion!

So to my proposal. What if we combined the goal of learning English with the hope of building bridges? What if at the very beginning of language training we were to say, "You may learn what makes us Americans"? To do this, I propose we incorporate the questions in our American citizenship test into our language training. With these questions as the basis for learning vocabulary, we would also be creating the basis for learning who we Americans are.

Imagine that you are teaching or taking an American-English language class. These could be themes for discussion not only about the language as such but also, and more importantly, what makes us Americans. These are actual questions from the new American naturalization test.

American Government

A. Principles of American Democracy

What is the supreme law of the land?

Answer: The Constitution

What does the Constitution do?

A: sets up the government; A: defines the government; A: protects basic rights of AmericansThe idea of self-government is in the first three words of the Constitution.

What are these words?

A: We the People

What is an amendment?

A: a change (to the Constitution); A: an addition (to the Constitution).

What do we call the first ten amendments to the Constitution?

A: The Bill of Rights

What did the Declaration of Independence do?

A: announced our independence (from Great Britain); A: declared our independence (from Great Britain); A: said that the United States is free (from Great Britain)

What are rights in the Declaration of Independence?

A: life; A: liberty; A: the pursuit of happiness.

What is freedom of religion?

A: You can practice any religion, or not practice a religion. There is no state religion in America; we cannot have a state religion.

What is the "rule of law"?

A: Everyone must follow the law; A: Leaders must obey the law; A: Government must obey the law; A: No one is above the law.

B. System of Government

*Name one branch or part of the government. ***

A: Congress: legislative; A: President: executive A: courts: judicial

What stops one branch of government from becoming too powerful?

A: checks and balances; A: separation of powers

What are two rights of everyone living in the United States?

A: freedom of expression; A: freedom of speech; A: freedom of assembly; A: freedom to petition the government; A: freedom of worship; A: the right to bear arms

What are two ways that Americans can participate in their democracy?

A: vote; A: join a political party; A: campaign; A: join a civic group; A: join a community group; A: give an elected official your opinion on an issue; A: Representatives; A: publicly support or oppose an issue or policy; A: run for office; A: write to a newspaper.

With this as a basis of American-English language study, imagine the great strides you will take toward understanding how Americans think. You will understand what words mean for them and will be able to discuss those themes, which make them who they are. This is important for any translator, for any diplomat, for any informed traveler to know.

Or you could consider historical questions and imagine again what avenues this discussion would open up.

Name one problem that led to the American Civil War.

A: slavery; A: economic reasons; A: states' rights

What did the Emancipation Proclamation do?

A: freed the slaves; A: freed slaves in the Confederacy; A: freed slaves in the Confederate states; A: freed slaves in most Southern states

What did Susan B. Anthony do?

A: fought for women's rights; A: fought for civil rights

Name two national U.S. holidays.

A: New Year's Day; A: Martin Luther King, Jr., Day; A: Presidents' Day; A: Memorial Day; A: Independence Day; A: Labor Day; A: Columbus Day; A: Veterans Day; A: Thanksgiving; A: Christmas

Discussions along these lines would lead naturally to observations about what Americans celebrate, why, and how. How Americans celebrate would in turn lead to lively conversations about what we consider part of our lives, such as the sport of baseball, the sport of American football, music like jazz, rock and roll, and folk music. Once someone completes the advanced American English class, they would have a good working knowledge not only of who these Americans are, but what is important to them.

Any country can do this with their language, or languages. This same idea can be applied to learn what it takes to become a Kazakh, or a Pole, or a member of any other land; the study of the language should address how one becomes a citizen of that country. We can understand the Kazakhs by learning about the ideas that are important to them, and so on throughout all the languages of the world. Language study would then truly build bridges. If we learn what the people of a country believe is important to them, through learning how they understand different words, then we have begun to build a bridge. These bridges help take away misunderstandings that might lead to difficulties. We can always walk over a bridge and ask for clarification; the bridge has only to be there.

Language classes that teach what is understood by various words can be of great value. How better to understand someone than to know what is meant by his concepts of the right, the good, the true, and the beautiful. A good place to start, as my presentation offers, is to learn the language associated with the national requirements for citizenship. With such a knowledgeable basis for dialogue, we can begin to build understanding and peace. And if you know how to bring peace, you are very rich indeed.

PART V: FEARS AND HOPES

Nothing in life is to be feared. It is only to be understood-- Marie Curie

Our future is not in stars but in our own minds and hearts. Creative leadership and liberal education, which in fact go together, are the first requirements for a hopeful future for humankind. Fostering these---leadership, learning, and empathy between cultures, was and remains the purpose of the international scholarship program that I was privileged to sponsor in the U.S. Senate over forty years ago. It is a modest program with an immodest aim---the achievement in international affairs of a regime more civilized, rational, and humane than the empty system of power of the past. I believed in that possibility when I began. I still do.-- J. William Fulbright, U.S. Senator, commenting on the Fulbright International Scholarship Program

Hope begins in the dark, the stubborn hope that if you just show up and try to do the right thing, the dawn will come.--Anne Lamott, **Bird by Bird**

DOING RIGHT

Americans like movies where truth speaks to power. Rest assured, however, power doesn't appreciate it, especially in this country. Joseph P. Kennedy, Ambassador to Great Britain in 1939, denounced the movie *Mr. Smith Goes to Washington*, by Frank Capra, as a scandal. It made foreigners believe "the United States is full of graft, corruption, and lawlessness." Ambassador Kennedy didn't want to upset the sensitivities of world leaders such as Adolf Hitler and Joseph Stalin. Average Americans, on the other hand, flocked to Capra's movie. They didn't delude themselves that we were perfect. They didn't fear letting the world know that American confidence could handle hard truths about themselves.

Americans live with paradox. On the one hand, we like ourselves. We see ourselves as special in the world, not bound by the dead hand of tradition. We consider those who point out our flaws as informers or worse. We have whole industries dedicated to drumming up our national identity as lone wolf, independent minded, patriotic, pragmatic folk. Yet we relish denouncing ourselves, too. We watch both the *Crucible* and *On the Waterfront*.

When Martin Luther King took a stand for Civil Rights in Birmingham, he was rewarded with jail time. Time proved him to have been right. Jonathan Pollard, on the other hand, secretly acted upon his belief that the United States should do more to help Israel. He had to be found out, was arrested as a spy, and imprisoned. Not all those who act upon their beliefs are moral heroes.

One thing that characterizes the moral advocate is a willingness to face the consequences of his actions, the better to bring an unjust system to light in America. We think of such people as John Brown, who believed in violence, and Daniel Ellsberg, who did not.

Better to consider the case of Richard Marven and Samuel Shaw. Marven was a junior officer and Shaw a midshipman under the command of Esek Hopkins. Hopkins was the definition of Colonial era power. He was no less than Commander of the Continental Navy whose brother was a signer of the Declaration of Independence. Further, he was a war hero, having beaten the mighty British Navy in combat. But he was also an alleged torturer of British prisoners. Marven and Shaw believed this wrong, and brought this to the attention of the new American government. Hopkins had them both arrested. Congress disagreed with Hopkins, and created the first law to state: "That it is the duty of all persons in the service of the United States, all well as all other inhabitants thereof, to give the earliest information to Congress or any other proper authority of any misconduct, frauds or other misdemeanors committed by any persons in the service of these states, which may come to their knowledge".

Hopkins, despite all the power, prestige, lawyers, military brass and politicians on his side, was defeated. Marven and Shaw, good officers who believed we were better than torturers, decided to act against wrongdoing in government. Moreover, they believed in our ability to correct ourselves. Marven and Shaw didn't run away.

GATEWAY TO AMERICA

The Lorrine Emery Award my wife Jane and I received from Global Ties, United States, was an inspiration to do more to open the gates of America to others. Global Ties is the non-profit organization that implements four US State Department exchange programs for foreign representatives. This National Award was given to us in recognition for our work with these delegations from all over the world. Significantly, over 110 years earlier my home city of St. Louis, Missouri, sponsored the Great 1904 World's Fair, the Louisiana Purchase Exposition. The theme of that fair was to introduce the idea of our city as a gateway to commerce, settlement, and citizenship. I never felt a greater love for my ancestors than when we won an award with the same goal for our country. I offer this commentary about that award.

One Handshake at a Time

The Lorrine Emery Award for citizen diplomacy means so much to Jane and me because we've always imagined our family as unofficial American ambassadors. We lived together overseas some thirteen-plus years. In fact, Jane spent most of her life overseas, learning what it means to experience the wonder of the new, and what it takes to understand and perhaps gain acceptance among the local people. Incidentally, her dad was in the regiment about which the television series *Band of Brothers* was made.

As Americans abroad, we've tried to orient our entire lives to represent our nation as it can be. We've worked with refugees in the Netherlands, counting some among our current friends. Jane gave demonstrations of American cooking and family traditions, and hosted foreign visitors in Italy. In Germany, we learned the language, sponsoring and befriending those we met who came over from the former East bloc. We tried to pave the way for better understanding and reconciliation of former enemies. Jane even organized a remarkably successful event in the Netherlands when she arranged a Native American weekend, drawing support from literally dozens of Native American soldiers. We tried to carry this joy of life with us to Alabama, my next assignment after the Cold War.

We volunteered with Global Ties, a non-profit organization which implements State Department exchange programs. We guide foreign guests to their appointments and try to treat each group as if they are the most important persons to visit Huntsville. We carefully review their biographies, and determine their particular interests, the better to make a personal connection. We've learned local history and prepare to answer visitors' questions. Many questions concern our Civil War or the civil rights period. We answer without equivocation. In fact, we make sure to tell our guests, before their formal meetings, to ask any question, and not be satisfied until the question is answered. Assume every issue is on the table. Jane is especially attentive to dietary or religious needs of our visitors, and conscientiously checks ahead for their particular requests. I should add all love their first chance to eat alligator!

Above all though, we've found that to study others' beliefs and customs makes us aware and respectful of cultural differences. Of most significance, and most commented upon, is our honest and straightforward method of dealing with questions. We try to respond to inquiries with comprehensiveness; to place information in context. We don't avoid even potentially problematic issues. We enjoy asking as well as answering questions! That's how we learn. Listening is a wonderful art, and expands our world. In fact, one guest, a mayor from the Philippines, reported later that the cooperative efforts he'd discovered here through Global Ties resulted in his peace initiative between combating factions in his country. They even worked together after a tremendous typhoon, helping each other regardless of ethnic or religious differences! Our motto is that of Abraham Lincoln, "If you would win a man to your cause, first convince him that you are his sincere friend." We've learned what patience, diligence, imagination, and sincere care for each other can do to break down age-old walls.

AMBASSADORS FOR AMERICA

This speech was presented by my wife Jane, to whom this book is dedicated. She gave this on the occasion of our winning the Lorinne Emery National Award for Volunteerism. The award was presented by Global Ties, United States, in Washington, DC. Global Ties is a non-profit organization that implements small US State Department programs which share information, culture, and capabilities with foreign visitors. These visits enhance foreign awareness of America, our practices, commerce, culture, and goals, and helps us to understand theirs. Thus Jane's life represents a case where America offered its best.

Thank you all so much for this great honor. No one is ever alone in the achievement of an award, of course. We've enjoyed the privilege of meeting so very many people who are working to make this world a better place. This includes not only our foreign guests, but the many Alabamians who work so selflessly as part of this program. I'd like to add too the wonderful Global Ties people we've met here as well.

I'm an "army brat" who traveled overseas for the first time when I was I was 18 months old. My dad was literally one of the Band of Brothers who helped liberate Europe from Nazi fascism, and I was a Cold Warrior without realizing it for years. I lived in Germany and remember hearing President Kennedy proclaim he was a Berliner. I remember when the Berlin Wall went up, and celebrated when it came down.

As Americans overseas my mom, dad, sister and I were the foreigners, but ambassadors, too, in some small way. Later with a family of my own we also filled that role for many years overseas. Sharing a picnic or playing with another kid who didn't speak your language, or smiling at a baby: these small everyday actions can bridge gaps we don't even know exist.

We've met people who were hidden during the Second World War and those who hid them, resistance workers and others jailed for "crimes against the state". Most were ordinary people, just like us.

Yet, some of the world's most life changing events happened because of unknown people who try to do good, by the lights they are given. That's how we try to represent America; to be a sign of what Americans can be, and what people can do, when we care about each other as a society, and as allies and friends. No one knows who invented the potter's wheel, but we know the inventor had to care about the future, about those who would come later. I like to meet my guests from abroad as someone who wants to listen, learn, and perhaps help. In this small way I want to build a happier future for us all.

So when I have the opportunity to meet and work with people from other countries, I try to do what President Kennedy asked of us those many years ago, "What can I do for my country"?

Thank you again for this honor.

I spoke after Jane.

Thank you for the incredibly kind hospitality you've shown Jane and me. I'd also like to thank especially the wonderful and supportive Global Ties staff in Alabama.

Let me echo Jane's comments of thanks and gratitude. And I'd like to add one more name to thank. I'd like to thank a kind and thoughtful high school teacher of mine, Mr. Ray Bruin. Mr. Bruin invited a couple of my McBride high school classmates and me, all those many years ago, to a presentation by Senator J. William Fulbright, then head of the Senate Foreign Relations Committee. I can't begin to remember all he said in the speech, now over forty-five years ago, but I remember his theme, 'Of the dangers of the arrogance of power.'

The dangers of the arrogance of power. This is a powerful thought. I had some 37 years in the federal government to reflect upon the truth of this idea, as our national efforts waxed and waned due to the assertion, or avoidance, of pride, arrogance, and unwarranted fears. One distilled concept has remained with me, though, which became remarkably, and consistently, clear as the years went by. This is true from dozens of conversations on this very subject with many foreigners, from many walks of life, over many years, conducted in several languages.

It was not our mighty army nor military; it was not our powerful industrial might, it wasn't even our financial wizardry which foreigners admired about us. What they admired, and again this is from people in all walks of life, what they admired about us is our fundamental idea that all men are created equal. Americans not only assert this, but try... and often fail... to make a society, with a government to support it, based on this very principle: that all men are created equal.

I sometimes think our ancestors from several generations ago understood this simple idea clearer than we do today. I saw in the Smithsonian Museum a Peace Medallion. This is a medal which our Presidents of the early 1800's would give to the mighty chiefs of the great tribes of our American West when they came to visit Washington. On one side was an engraving of the face of the President. The President represented what we believed ourselves to be. On the other side, engraved at the top of the medallion, was the word, "Peace".

Peace. At some elementary level, isn't that what all our government's actions hope to accomplish? Domestic tranquility? Yes, we know we've so often sadly failed, but there it is. Peace. A goal we hope to achieve. And how were we going to achieve this?

Around the lower side of the medal was the word Friendship. Not armies, not industrial might, but friendship. We can all understand this word. We all understand at some level that friendship means you and I are equal. We listen to one another. We try our best to be truthful.

I was astounded to hear today, almost as a side comment at our Voice of America visit, that almost every foreign guest took a photograph of the Voice of America Charter, carved in metal on the wall. This simple assertion, that the news should be truth, is a revolutionary concept in places where the press is not free. We often forget freedom of the press. Honesty opens the door to friendship. We respect others when we seek to understand them. Friendship. We act humbly, without the arrogance of power.

And then in the center of the Peace Medallion, there was a carving of two hands clasping, in friendship. Something the simplest person can understand. Peace through friendship. When I discovered that Global Ties' symbol showed the clasped hands of friendship, I knew this was a place for me; where we could influence peace, one handshake at a time. Thank you, ladies and gentlemen, for your kindness and thoughtful gift to us.

WATCHING THE WATCHERS

When I was a little boy, one of my fun things to do was to read a random story from the encyclopedia with grandma. I recall vividly how she showed me a series of pictures of causes of the American Revolution. One showed a British soldier inside a private colonial home.

"He could just come in, even if you didn't ask him to?"

"Yes," grandma said, "whenever he wanted."

This struck me as very wrong. Very wrong indeed.

On the floor of the Massachusetts colony Superior Court, a young man rose to denounce an act with the benign title, 'writ of assistance'. This writ allowed British customs officials to enter any home, any time, for little or no cause, in search of smuggled goods. It had been the favorite sport of American colonials to dodge British taxes. Smuggling was as American as the turkey. Yet as the cost of the American wars against the French and Indians consumed vast amounts of British money, soldiers, and equipment, such American underhandedness would have to be stopped.

The London government finally said "enough". Smuggling would be stopped. They were going to control the borders. They'd enforce tax collection to pay for the colonials' own protection against the existential threat of French and Indian terror. Indeed such 'writs of assistance' would break smuggling, secure tax payment, and pay for that protection. It was all for the colonials' own good. In fact, the law was well intended. Officials of the Crown were trying to do right by finding a way to pay for the war against the French and Indians by making violators pay taxes.

James Otis, Jr., a Boston lawyer, in an impassioned appeal, observed the real effects of such a fine- sounding law. He noted that any unelected customs official had, per the 'writ of assistance', the right to come into any home to search for smuggled goods. Whereas English law had stated before that there was no right of anyone to enter into a home without probable cause, without a judge's permission, and without specifying what was being sought, now the 'writ of assistance' was overriding that. In fact, the writ was universal, and applied to everyone, not a specified individual suspected of something. Worse, it was perpetual; it was valid forever. "…a person with this writ may enter all houses, shops, etc. at will and command all to assist him." For "Everyone with this writ may be a tyrant… (such) a man is accountable to no person for his doings."

Otis thus denounced this violation of the ancient Anglo-Saxon right to peaceful security in one's home. "A man's house is his castle; and while he is quiet he is as secure as a prince in his castle." No law could presume him guilty, make him prove his innocence, nor allow random violations of his peace.

Otis's speech was carefully listened to that long-ago February day in 1761. One man in particular was observed taking many notes. John Adams, who went on to be a formulator of the Constitution, scribbled away so as to remember this legal principle. Otis's ideas were later taken as a basis for the Fourth Amendment to that Constitution. That amendment is instructive:

"The right of the people to be secure in their persons, houses, papers, and effects, against unreasonable searches and seizures, shall not be violated, and no Warrants shall issue, but upon probable cause, supported by Oath or affirmation, and particularly describing the place to be searched, and the persons or things to be seized."

Even the best intentions of government must be regulated. There must be serious, authoritative, open, and known oversight of all laws, even the most well intentioned. This is because we accept that any man can be, or may become, malevolent, petty, manipulative, or vindictive. Power is an addictive drug. It is, after all, why we inserted the balance of powers in the Constitution. For no man is pure, no man is beyond temptation. Good people in government will gladly accept oversight, will welcome public scrutiny, and limitation of their powers. Such is for the greater good, the natural right of people to be secure in their 'persons, houses, papers, and effects'.

As we sit in our homes this frigid winter, let's remember this great debate of that February long ago. To do so renders the great controversies of today much clearer. To know why and how such amendments came about helps make today's debates no longer seem so complex, not so complex at all.

Good and Bad Government

On the great cupola of the Swiss Federal Palace, written in an archaic script surrounding the colorful district crests of the several states, there is the motto, "One for all, and all for one". This theme has been a daily, visible guide for lawmakers for over a century. It echoes that most famous mural found in the city hall of Siena, Italy. There, the city councilors are even today surrounded by the allegories of good and bad government, painted by Ambrogio Lorenzetti in the 1340s.

In the recent furor of our own election process, I paused to reflect on why we have a government. What is it that we hope for as a result of all the elections? Victory? What, though, does victory mean? What does the result of victory look like? What should our elected leaders think about as they assume their new positions?

The result of good government in Lorenzetti's mural, visible to all, is peace, prosperous pursuits, and celebration. There is the quiet, daily peace characterized by openness, protected by honest laws and well-disciplined soldiers. Justice ensures that rulers, judges, and tradesmen are fair; that decisions are based on magnanimity, prudence, and wisdom. The viewer can see honest tradesmen pursuing their work as weavers, wool shearers, and masons in colorful open shops. The safe atmosphere of the town allows the weakest among the community, women and children, to dance and enjoy life without fear. The orderly, bounteous countryside is bursting with grains, tended to by hardy yeomen. A real sense of community prevails because everyone has a part, a distinct part, that nevertheless supports the greater good. In the distance, the city gates are open to hearty, well-dressed traders arriving and departing with cornucopias of goods. The city shares its own prosperity by going out to exchange the fruits of honest labor. The common good is served in a well-maintained city, surrounded by a bounteous countryside. Virtue is seen as what is best for all. Cooperation, community, compromise, and solidarity mark good government and the citizens who support it.

Bad government is also visible. There darkness prevails. It is lawless; even men are not safe on the streets. Random, unaccounted-for people prowl, accost others, and carry weapons. It is every man for himself. The government seems to exist for private gain. Money pays for private defense of apparent wealth amidst poverty. Lorenzetti shows us women as a commodity, not a part of the community. No sense of community exists where doors are barred shut, the city is a barricaded against thieves and invaders. The atmosphere is fear in a grim, empty, lonely town. Everyone is shut up inside their own dwelling, for no one can call the obvious depiction of a fortress their home. Even the countryside is bereft of people. Fields are fallow. The sky is dark over a lonely, distant, fortified castle keep. The absence of farm folk has killed the fields just as much as warfare, which marks its presence in the burned houses and random, stalking soldiery who seem intent on plunder and rape.

I recall a mural in Indiana where a contemporary figure held the scales of justice. On one side was a bag of money, on the other an empty place where another scale should have been. Instead, where the scale would have hung, there was a metal head; there was nothing below it. The money was the price of the head, and the lack of a scale showed that the money had bought his soul, too.

So we should think about these things that other societies, in other times, have thought about and depicted so well. What would we put up to remind our own elected officials why they are there? I know my choice would be to engrave over their office door, "One for all, and all for one." When we don't remember that, we get bad government. We belong to one another; we're all in this together.

Terrain Walk With My Little Boy

You see those pines and hardwoods over there beside the field?
On a terrain walk we called them a tree line.
That's because we would line the cannons along the edge of the forest,
The better to hide from view, but still be able to fire in the direction we wanted.

A turn on the path like this is where we set up 'L-shaped ambushes'.
This way we'd kill all the enemy, no matter which direction he ran,
But wouldn't shoot each other in the night when we sprang the trap on them.

Often we'd set up our machine guns in places where they could cover one another,
Like those two knolls, there and over there. We called this overlapping fields of fire.

And that stone tower in the town down there was to be blown over to slow down tanks.

We called this hill OP 3. There once was an observation post here.
From here I was to call in artillery, if ever the balloon went up. From right here.

You can't imagine how grateful I am you never had to waste your life learning all this.

Now those trees will forever be only dark green, mysterious, and beautiful; the knolls places where kids can sled or run.

And you can find out what unexpected discovery is beyond the bend in this pleasant road.

Maybe you can find out what the locals named these hills; maybe for ancient gods or mighty kings?

And you and your kids can hear the bells of that stone church tower if you walk through the town, on your way over to play with the kids on the other side.

HOPE IN TIME OF RUMORS OF WAR

I write in all humility of spirit, in the desperate hope that somehow it may be of use in the forlorn and seemingly hopeless fight against war.--
Kerr Eby, American Soldier and Artist, World War I

My Uncle Barrett, who was in the navy in the Second World War, thought of it this way. "If Truman didn't drop the bomb, there's a good chance we'd all be dead." He'd experienced firsthand "..Kamikaze suicide pilots who flew at our ship while we fired pompom guns at them. Even when we hit them, instead of bailing out they came straight ahead and crashed like a bomb into our ship." What he meant was an invasion of the Japanese home islands would have probably cost over a million American dead, not to mention untold Japanese. Odds are, if we invaded, I might not be here either, because my own dad was enroute to the Pacific.

I've consulted the greatest minds that ever wrote for the answer to one question. How do you defeat evil, if not at least accepting the possibility of an ultimate appeal to violence? Of course, I'd assumed all peaceful means have been tried first. Then what? I've inquired of the some of the finest minds who've ever studied this only to find that this mystifies them, too. Absolute pacifism hasn't worked. Peaceful resistance has been, however, remarkably successful. Gandhi, Martin Luther King, Jr., and the Solidarity union in Poland demonstrated this on the grand scale. In the end, such resistance wins, but the price to be paid before that day comes will be horrific, painful, and require many, many accommodations indeed. I can state, as a truism I've discovered, that most of those who have truly known war's bloody and mindless slaughter, are those who most ardently seek an earlier peaceful solution. Even once a war starts, no chance for reconciliation should be passed by. Be it through diplomacy, negotiation, or more imaginative attempts at reconciliation, or outside mediation, it is always best to honestly try to give peace a chance.

I spent my career in the Army, and in the Army's Civil Service. In the end, I was haunted by the thought that what we really trusted was not God, but our nuclear bombs to protect us. We were whistling in the dark past the cemetery that somehow we'd avoid a war, but thought we'd be the winners if one came. Yet, John F. Kennedy was right to comment that the fruits of victory in a nuclear war would be ashes in our mouth. Now the world engages in 'small wars'. We often see individuals who dream of mass murder to make some cause or other known. We've arrived at the dead end of murder for publicity's sake. A man with a bomb is judge, jury, and executioner. *Sic transit gloria mundi.* How fragile our civilization is that some perceive every wrong, true or imagined, as something only to be dealt with by a trigger pull or a flipped switch on a suicide vest.

I've been attracted to Abraham Lincoln's wry observation that he would destroy an enemy if he made him his friend. And yet, our great Civil War showed that dream faded, too. There are always those who would not stop, think, make slow and arduous accommodations, and compromise. Rather, many risk all in a war. This is the test for all generations; how can we not be so afraid? How do we overcome our fear of the other that makes us expect the worst? Why do we always trust our heavy weaponry to protect us, when an ounce of imaginative human outreach is never even tried? What can we do to stop before we get to the many-tiered collapsed hotel of wretched death, pitiless war, and moonscape ruin? Just a visit to a memorial is not enough to remind us. The names of those murdered in a bombing, a misbegotten retaliation, or a judicial killing cannot efface our anguish that we were unable to prevent the cause of their deaths in the first place.

And yet I still believe we can prevent the next war. I smile at the brilliance of a friend who only half in jest said those in the national military services should get a bonus for every year there is no war. It is astounding but true; I've met former East German and Czech soldiers who, in war, would have been my 'mortal enemies'. Instead, after the peaceful end of the Cold War and the dismantlement of the Iron Curtain, we've shared camaraderie and conviviality, enjoying one another's families.

My favorite scene in any movie was in the 1936 film *Dawn Patrol*.
David Niven and Erroll Flynn, two British World War I flyers, shoot
down a German pilot who is captured. They meet him at their officers'
club upon landing. All three drink themselves drunk, and together
plan a zany song-filled motorcycle romp across the French countryside.
A guard stops them as they are leaving the club, arm in arm, singing
merrily away. "Excuse me sir, but that man's a German!" he declares,
weapon lowered. "A German?" say bleary-eyed Niven and Flynn, "But
he can sing!"

I wish we could all find out, before it is too late, that those we fear can
sing, just like we can.

Even When All Seems Lost, There's Hope

On a chilly fall afternoon, on the town square of a typical Southern town called Athens, Alabama, a not-so typical event took place. Residents inspired by local officers of the court gathered to commemorate one of their profession who stood against the majority in a time of racial hatred. The event at the Athens State University Learning Center commemorated a stunning and courageous decision, 83 years ago. In those Depression-ridden, fearful and hateful years when World War II was in the offing, a courageous act was performed by Judge James Horton because it was the right thing to do. He decided to overturn the death sentence of one of the Scottsboro Boys and order a retrial. The Scottsboro boys were nine black youths who had been falsely accused of rape by two white women. The case was wrought with public prejudice of those who brought the sentence, hatred by vocal Klansmen, and racial malice, not to mention threats of lynching. In the face of all this, Judge Horton cancelled the jury's decision for the death penalty and demanded a retrial. For this he himself received death threats, "Your life ain't worth a nothing." And he lost his position. Now, generations later, he will be honored in Athens with a cast statue on the town square.

I hope this quotation from Judge Horton is on the base of the Statue:

"The world at this time and in many lands is showing intolerance and hate. It seems sometimes that love has almost deserted the human bosom. It seems that only hate has taken its place. It is only for a time gentlemen, because it is the great things in life, God's great principles, matters of eternal right, that alone live. Wrong dies and truth forever lasts, and we should have faith in that."

Judge James Horton, who will live in our hearts forever, was a good man who did the right thing, even when it was dangerous to do so.

GOOD AT HEART

It's difficult in times like these: ideals, dreams and cherished hopes rise within us, only to be crushed by grim reality. It's a wonder I haven't abandoned all my ideals, they seem so absurd and impractical. Yet I cling to them because I still believe, in spite of everything, that people are truly good at heart.-- Anne Frank, **Diary of a Young Girl,** murdered by Nazis at Bergen-Belsen Concentration Camp, 1945

*Truth and love will overcome lies and hatred.--*Vaclav Havel, Poet, Playwright, and Political Dissident who became the first President of a Free Czechoslovakia after the fall of the Communist dictatorship.

- The End

About the Author:

John William Davis is a retired US Army counterintelligence officer, civil servant, and linguist. He was commissioned from Washington University in St. Louis as an artillery officer in the 101st Air Assault Division. Thereafter, he went into counterintelligence and served some 37 years. A linguist, Mr. Davis learned foreign languages in each country he served.

As a consequence of the Cold War and its bitter aftermath he wrote *Rainy Street Stories, 'Reflections on Secret Wars, Terrorism, and Espionage'*. He wanted to reveal not only true events, but also the moral and ethical impact of the secret world on real people. With the publication of *Around the Corner*, Davis expands his reflections on conflicted human nature to our present day traumas of fear, and causes for hope.

To contact John, visit redbikepublishing.com or send an e-mail to: author@redbikepublishing.com

A special word of thanks and a favor to ask

Thank you for buying my book. I really appreciate you being a reader and hope you find it helpful. If you have any questions, please feel free to contact me.

I would really love to hear your feedback. Your input would help to make my future books better. Please leave a helpful review, where you purchased your book, of what you thought of it.

I would also ask that you let a friend know about the book as well.

Thanks so much and best of success to you!! All the best:

John

If you liked *Around the Corner*, please read my other book, *Rainy Street Stories.*